# STRONG KIDS

Grades
3–5

 **STRONG KIDS**™

Other programs in **Strong Kids**™:
A Social & Emotional Learning Curriculum

*Strong Start—Grades K–2:*
*A Social & Emotional Learning Curriculum*

*Strong Kids—Grades 6–8:*
*A Social & Emotional Learning Curriculum*

*Strong Teens—Grades 9–12:*
*A Social & Emotional Learning Curriculum*

# STRONG KIDS

Grades 3–5

## A Social & Emotional Learning Curriculum

by

**Kenneth W. Merrell, Ph.D.**
University of Oregon

with assistance from

Dianna Carrizales, Ph.D.

Laura Feuerborn, Ph.D.

Barbara A. Gueldner, Ph.D.

and

Oanh K. Tran, Ph.D.

·P·A·U·L·H·
BROOKES
PUBLISHING CO.®

Baltimore • London • Sydney

**Paul H. Brookes Publishing Co.**
Post Office Box 10624
Baltimore, Maryland 21285-0624

www.brookespublishing.com

Typeset by Barton Matheson Willse & Worthington, Baltimore, Maryland.
Manufactured in the United States of America by
Versa Press, Inc., East Peoria, Illinois.

**Library of Congress Cataloging-in-Publication Data**
Merrell, Kenneth W.
   Strong start : a social and emotional learning curriculum / by Kenneth W. Merrell,
   Danielle M. Parisi, and Sara A. Whitcomb.
      p.   cm.
   Vols. 2–4 have the title: Strong kids
   Vols. 2–4 authored by Kenneth W. Merrell alone.
   Includes bibliographical references.
   ISBN-13: 978-1-55766-929-2 (v. 1 : layflat (paper)
   ISBN-10: 1-55766-929-5 (v. 1 : layflat (paper)
   ISBN-13: 978-1-55766-930-8 (v. 2 : layflat (paper)
   ISBN-10: 1-55766-930-9 (v. 2 : layflat (paper)
   [etc.]
   1. Affective education.   2. Social learning.   3. Child development.   4. Emotional intelligence.
   5. Education—Social aspects.   I. Parisi, Danielle M.   II. Whitcomb, Sara A.   III. Title.
   IV. Title: Strong kids.

   LB1072.M47 2007
   370.15'34—dc22
                                                    2007015480

British Library Cataloguing in Publication data are available from the British Library.

# Contents

**Section I   Introduction and Overview**

**Section II   The *Strong Kids—Grades 3–5* Curriculum**

# Contents of the Accompanying CD-ROM

About the Author
Contributors
About This CD-ROM

**Lesson 1**
Supplement 1.1: *Strong Kids* Lessons
Supplement 1.2: *Strong Kids* Rules
Supplement 1.3: Introducing *Strong Kids*

**Lesson 2**
Supplement 2.1: Definitions
Supplement 2.2: Feelings Identification
Supplement 2.3: How Do You Feel?
Supplement 2.4: About My Feelings

**Lesson 3**
Supplement 3.1: Ways of Showing Feelings 1
Supplement 3.2: Ways of Showing Feelings 2
Supplement 3.3: Practice Situations
Supplement 3.4: Practice Application
Supplement 3.5: Reacting to Emotional Situations

**Lesson 4**
Supplement 4.1: Definitions
Supplement 4.2: Definitions of the Anger Model
Supplement 4.3, Option A: The Anger Model (Negative Example)
Supplement 4.3, Option B: The Anger Model (Negative Example)
Supplement 4.4: Anger Control Skills
Supplement 4.5: Negative and Positive Examples
Supplement 4.6: Anger Management Worksheet

**Lesson 5**
Supplement 5.1: Definitions
Supplement 5.2: Emotions
Supplement 5.3: Small-Group Student Role Plays
Supplement 5.4: Empathy Assignment

**Lesson 6**
Supplement 6.1: Feelings Thermometer
Supplement 6.2: Common Thinking Errors
Supplement 6.3: Situations
Supplement 6.4: Homework Assignment

**Lesson 7**
Supplement 7.1: Common Thinking Errors
Supplement 7.2: Evidence For or Against
Supplement 7.3: Reframing Negative Thoughts
Supplement 7.4: Changing Thinking Errors
Supplement 7.5: Feelings Thermometer
Supplement 7.6: Changing Thinking Errors

**Lesson 8**
Supplement 8.1: Definitions
Supplement 8.2: The ABCDE Model of Learned Optimism
Supplement 8.3: Cartoon Situation
Supplement 8.4: Let's Talk About What We Know

**Lesson 9**
Supplement 9.1: Definitions
Supplement 9.2: Alternatives to Conflict
Supplement 9.3: Problem-Solving Model
Optional Supplement: Role-Play Activities
Supplement 9.4: Resolving Conflicts

**Lesson 10**
Supplement 10.1: Definitions
Supplement 10.2: Let Go of Stress!
Supplement 10.3: Letting Go of Stress

**Lesson 11**
Supplement 11.1: Definitions
Supplement 11.2: Steps to Goal Attainment
Supplement 11.3: Personal Goal Organizer

**Lesson 12**
Supplement 12.1: Lessons We've Learned from *Strong Kids*

**Appendix**
Supplement A.1: Lessons from *Strong Kids*
Supplement A.2: The Situations and Feelings List
Supplement A.3: Discussion Questions

# About the Author

**Kenneth W. Merrell, Ph.D.,** is a professor of school psychology in the Department of Special Education and Clinical Sciences at the University of Oregon. He has served as School Psychology Program Director and Co-director as well as Department Head. Dr. Merrell received his Ph.D. in school psychology from the University of Oregon in 1998 and held tenured faculty positions at the University of Iowa and Utah State University before returning to the University of Oregon in 2001. In addition to his academic experience, he worked for 3 years as a school psychologist for a public school district and has extensive additional experience in providing psychological services and consultation in schools.

Dr. Merrell's research and scholarly work in social-emotional assessment and intervention in schools has been published widely in the field of school psychology, and he has been recognized in three separate studies as one of the 20 most influential scholars in the field over the past two decades. His peers have acknowledged his impact by electing him a fellow in the American Psychological Association's Division of School Psychology and Society for Clinical Child and Adolescent Psychology. His research studies have been published in *School Psychology Review*, *School Psychology Quarterly*, *Psychology in the Schools*, *Journal of Psychoeducational Assessment*, and elsewhere, and he has been interviewed for articles appearing in popular media, including *U.S. News & World Report*, *Family Circle*, and other national publications.

In addition to authoring more than 85 journal articles, Dr. Merrell has authored eight books and several assessment tools. Currently, Dr. Merrell serves as editor of Guilford Press's influential *Practical Intervention in the Schools* book series and is a member of the editorial advisory board for *School Psychology Review*. He is also a member of the Board of Directors at the Oregon Social Learning Center in Eugene.

## CONTRIBUTORS

**Dianna Carrizales, Ph.D.,** is an educational and assessment specialist at the Oregon Department of Education. She facilitates the statewide assessment options for students with disabilities. Dr. Carrizales graduated from the school psychology doctoral program at the University of Oregon in June of 2006 with a master's degree in special education and a doctorate in school psychology. She is currently licensed as a school psychologist in Oregon. Dr. Carrizales has been involved with the Oregon Resiliency Project since 2001 and has been involved with individual assessments, surveys, and assessment scales since her employment with Harcourt Assessment in 1998.

**Laura Feuerborn, Ph.D.,** is an assistant professor in special education at the University of Washington, Tacoma. She received her doctorate in school psychology from the University of Oregon and is a nationally certified school psychologist. Her research interests include school-wide systems reform, formative assessments, social-emotional learning tools, and early intervention programs for students at risk.

**Barbara A. Gueldner, Ph.D.,** is a visiting assistant professor in the school psychology program at the University of Oregon. She received her doctorate in school psychology from the University of Oregon and completed a clinical internship in pediatric psychology at The Children's Hospital in Denver, Colorado. Dr. Gueldner has 10 years experience as a school psychologist working in the public school system in Wisconsin and Oregon and is pursuing research in the area of universal prevention and early intervention of children's mental health concerns. Additional areas of interest include issues in pediatric psychology, consultation with educational and medical professionals, and training future psychologists.

**Oanh K. Tran, Ph.D.,** is an assistant professor of child clinical/school psychology at California State University, East Bay. She received her doctorate in school psychology from the University of Oregon in 2007. Dr. Tran completed her predoctoral internship at a community mental health agency working with children and youth with emotional and behavioral disorders. Her research interests include promoting social and emotional learning through teaching resiliency skills for the prevention and early intervention of mental health problems, behavioral consultation and assessment, and parent–child interactions. She has numerous years of experience working with diverse and at-risk populations in public and nonpublic schools as well as residential, foster care, outpatient, and in-home settings.

# Foreword

Since the 1990s, there has been an intense national focus on the mental health needs of children and youth. Increasing numbers of school-age youth are experiencing serious stress, anxiety, and depressive disorders. It is currently estimated that approximately 20%–25% of today's youth have mental health conditions that would result in a diagnosable mental disorder; yet, only about 20% of these youth will actually gain access to mental health services to address their problems. Furthermore, about 75% of these services will be obtained through the public schools.

It is clear that the ability of traditional mental health systems and their delivery mechanisms to solve this continuing problem is inadequate. We urgently need to find ways to promote and provide quality mental health–type services that are universal in nature, low cost, feasible, and easily accessible and that provide effective tools.

The development of the field of *social-emotional learning* offers great promise for addressing this set of issues within the context of schooling. This specialty shows that social-emotional learning processes are of parallel importance as academic learning processes and that they can have a powerful impact on both academic and social-emotional outcomes. I regard the Strong Kids™ curriculum (which includes *Strong Start*, *Strong Kids—Grades 3–5*, *Strong Kids—Grades 6–8*, and *Strong Teens*) as a model exemplar of effective social-emotional learning practices in teaching critical social-emotional concepts and coping skills, including self-regulation.

The Strong Kids curriculum is *practical*, *easy-to-use*, *low cost*, and *teacher friendly*. Perhaps of equal importance, it fits well into the normal routines of schooling and thus does not disrupt the instructional scope and sequence of most classrooms. This program is evidence based and of proven effectiveness.

The Strong Kids program is also highly flexible in that it targets both universal prevention goals and outcomes and also provides more intensive, targeted procedures for individual students who do not respond well to the program's classwide instructional approach. The Strong Kids curriculum is developmentally sequenced into four levels—Grades K–2, Grades 3–5, Grades 6–8, and Grades 9–12—thus covering the full K–12 age range. The Strong Kids program can also be used as part of a tier 3, tertiary-level comprehensive intervention program for students with the most severe mental health involvements.

I am impressed with the evidence so far of the Strong Kids program's efficacy. A series of recently completed studies document high levels of consumer satisfaction, social validity, and increases in social-emotional knowledge among students who have been exposed to it.

I strongly recommend this program for use in K–12 schools to address the social-emotional and mental health needs of today's students—many of whom bring serious, unsolved problems with them from outside the school setting, which can powerfully affect their in-school performance and behavior. These problems are not of the schools' making, but educators can play a very important role in addressing and ameliorating their more deleterious effects. I think the

Strong Kids curriculum is a seminal contribution to the field in improving our collective ability to intervene and prevent many of these problems.

*Hill M. Walker, Ph.D.*
*Director, Center on Human Development*
*University of Oregon*

# Acknowledgments

We would like to acknowledge other members of our research group who contributed to the development of *Strong Kids—Grades 3–5:* Leah Benazzi, Sara Castro-Olivo, Erin Chaparro, Christine Davis, Keith Herman, Duane Isava, Travis Laxton, Verity Levitt, Kelly McGraw, Kent McIntosh, Jean Mercier, Nicole Nakayama, Christiane Oilar, Kristin Orton, Scott Ross, Lisa Sterling, and Wendy Reinke.

# Introduction and Overview

# 1

# About *Strong Kids—Grades 3–5*

Strong Kids™: A Social and Emotional Learning Curriculum consists of four brief and practical social and emotional learning (SEL) programs that were designed for the purpose of teaching social and emotional skills, promoting resilience, strengthening assets, and increasing the coping skills of children and adolescents. This chapter provides some background information about children's mental health and social-emotional development, as well as a comprehensive overview of *Strong Kids—Grades 3–5*, the second volume in the Strong Kids curriculum. It provides tips for using the curriculum effectively and with confidence. *Strong Kids—Grades 3–5* is designed specifically for use with children in Grades 3–5, or approximately ages 8–12. Because *Strong Kids—Grades 3–5* is designed to be both a prevention and an early intervention program, it has a wide range of applications and may be used effectively with high-functioning, typically developing, and at-risk children, as well as children with emotional disturbance. It can also be used in a variety of settings.

Children in the *Strong Kids—Grades 3–5* target range face some unique challenges related to social and emotional development. As they progress from the primary grades to the intermediate grades, they begin to receive more academic specialization and may feel pressure associated with specialized learning as they move into subject matter instruction at school. At the same time, they must adapt to negotiating an increased number of social situations as they begin to interact with more children, have more teachers at school, and take on more complex social tasks. As children in this age range begin to mature cognitively, they become increasingly aware of some of the challenges they face. Issues that children may have been previously unaware of or only partially aware of—such as family stresses, marital conflict of parents, acceptance or rejection by peers, and expectations at school and in their community—may become increasingly clear to them. In addition, many children in Grades 3–5 live in communities or families where they are exposed to ineffective or inappropriate models for solving conflict and dealing with problems. *Strong Kids—Grades 3–5* is designed to help teach children the skills to negotiate these issues while having fun and engaging in activities that support their academic learning.

## DESIGN OF THE STRONG KIDS CURRICULUM

We designed the Strong Kids curriculum to target each of the five pathways to wellness advocated by Cowen (1994), a pioneer in the modern science of mental health prevention and wellness promotion:

- Forming wholesome early attachments

- Acquiring age-appropriate competencies

- Having exposure to settings that favor wellness outcomes

- Having the empowering sense of being in control of one's fate

- Coping effectively with stress

Furthermore, as we created this curriculum over a 5-year period and then continued to refine and research it, we envisioned Strong Kids as a carefully designed SEL program to prevent the development of certain mental health problems and promote social and emotional wellness among young people. Strong Kids is not the right SEL program for all types of problems. We especially targeted the domain of internalizing behavioral and emotional problems (e.g., depression, anxiety, social withdrawal, somatic problems) and the promotion of what we term *social and emotional resiliency* in designing this curriculum: We never intended Strong Kids to be a comprehensive program for preventing school violence or antisocial behavior, even though it may play a role in supporting these aims as part of a comprehensive program of effective behavior support.

In addition, we specifically designed Strong Kids as a low-cost, low-technology program that can be implemented in a school or related educational setting with minimal professional training and resources. It is not necessary to be a licensed mental health professional to learn and implement this curriculum. It can also be taught in a self-contained manner within a specific environment and does not require expensive community wrap-around services or mandatory parent training groups.

The advantage of this programming approach is that Strong Kids is brief, efficient, skill-based, portable, and focused. One disadvantage of this approach is that the program is not designed to be a complete mental health treatment package for children and youth with severe mental health problems. Although our research to date has shown that the curriculum can make a meaningful difference with such populations, it should be used as one component of a comprehensive, intensive intervention program in such cases.

As mentioned previously, the *Strong Kids—Grades 3–5* program is aimed for use with children in the late primary and intermediate elementary grades. For younger or older students, the Strong Kids curriculum includes other developmentally appropriate programs for use throughout the K–12 grade span. *Strong Start* is for use with children in Grades K–2. *Strong Kids—Grades 6–8* is for use with students in middle school, and *Strong Teens* is for use with high school–age students, those in Grades 9–12 or at similar age ranges.

There are several appropriate settings for use of *Strong Kids—Grades 3–5*, including, but not limited to, general and special education classrooms, group counseling settings, and youth treatment facilities that have an educational component.

A wide range of professionals may appropriately serve as group leaders or instructors for this curriculum. General and special education teachers, speech-language pathologists, school counselors, social workers, psychologists, and other education or mental health professionals may serve as effective group leaders.

## FEASIBILITY AND EASE OF IMPLEMENTATION

This curriculum was developed with both time feasibility and ease of implementation as high priorities. Even an exceptionally strong intervention program will fail to make an impact if its time requirements and difficulty of implementation result in few people being able to use it within the time and training constraints of a school system or other youth-serving agency. Thus, the maximum duration of the curriculum is 12 weeks (if lessons are taught once per week), and the average length of each lesson is approximately 45–50 minutes.

One of the advantages of the Strong Kids curriculum is that it is designed to support academic skills and to be implemented *seamlessly* within an instructional program. The skills needed to effectively teach students academic skills are the same skills needed to deliver this curriculum effectively. Group leaders do not need to be mental health specialists or therapists. The activities in this curriculum not only promote social and emotional learning and resiliency but also support literacy, language arts, social studies, and health.

*Strong Kids—Grades 3–5* is a highly structured and partially scripted curriculum designed to cover very specific objectives and goals. We developed the objectives and goals for each lesson, as well as the implementation guidelines, based on current research findings in education and psychology, aiming for a prevention and intervention program that is built on a solid base of empirical evidence. Each lesson follows a similar format. The lessons provide optional scripts to aid concept delivery, sample situations and examples to better illustrate the concept, and opportunities for guided and independent practice. Group leaders can follow the script and examples directly or modify the lessons to utilize creativity.

We recommend teaching the *Strong Kids—Grades 3–5* lessons once per week for 12 weeks, although it is possible to effectively teach the curriculum at a more accelerated tempo such as two lessons per week for 6 weeks. The one lesson per week format will allow students sufficient time to complete homework assignments, internalize the concepts taught, and practice the new skills they learn, both at school and outside of school. We recommend that teachers and group leaders look for opportunities throughout the instructional day and the school week to support the learning that takes place during the *Strong Kids—Grades 3–5* lessons. Our experience, and that of many teachers and mental health professionals who have used the Strong Kids curriculum, is that it is easy to find opportunities to reinforce curriculum concepts, allow students to practice, and apply key concepts to everyday situations.

## PROMOTING CHILDREN'S MENTAL HEALTH

The primary mission of public education has traditionally been perceived as promoting the development of academic skills. There is no question that most educators, parents, students, and the general public also support and expect a broader mission for schools (Greenberg et al., 2003). Some examples of this expanded agenda include character education, development of good work habits, promotion of good citizenship, development of social and emotional competence, and promotion of healthy and productive lifestyle.

Commenting on the need for this broader agenda, Greenberg and his colleagues stated

> High-quality education should teach young people to interact in socially skilled and respectful ways; to practice positive, safe, and healthy behaviors; to contribute ethically and responsibly to their peer group, family, school, and community; and to possess basic competencies, work habits, and values as a foundation for meaningful employment and citizenship . . . . We consequently assert that school-based prevention programming—based on coordinated social, emotional, and academic learning—should be fundamental to preschool through high school education. (2003, pp. 466–467)

We emphatically agree with this statement. In addition, we propose that teaching young people positive social, emotional, and behavioral skills is not only an essential mission for educators and mental health professionals but also one of the most critical challenges facing our society in the 21st century.

As many researchers, writers, and public officials have noted, changes in the structure of society and families have resulted in an increasing percentage of children and families who are at risk for developing a variety of behavioral, social, and mental health problems (e.g., Costello & Angold, 2000; Doll & Lyon, 1998; Farmer & Farmer, 1999; Hoagwood & Erwin, 1997; Satcher, 1999). The numbers of children and youth affected by these problems are surprisingly high. Greenberg, Domitrovich, and Bumbarger (2001) have asserted that between 12% and 22% of children and adolescents younger than age 18 experience mental health problems of sufficient severity to be in need of mental health services. These percentages represent a staggering figure of up to 1 out of every 5 children and adolescents in some instances. Without question, effective responses to these problems, including mental health prevention and early intervention curricula in educational settings, must occur if these challenges are to be stemmed.

Despite sincere and well-meaning attempts to offer real solutions to social, emotional, and mental health problems of students in school settings, many of the programs or interventions that have been implemented are simply ineffective. Walker stated that "educators are notorious for embracing programs that look good but do no actual good" (2001, p. 2). In these educators' defense, we should note that school personnel who work on the front lines of serving children and youth who have significant mental health issues are often overworked and not provided with sufficient resources with which to make the impact they desire. Furthermore, some developers and publishers of mental health prevention programs tend to overwhelm educators and clinicians with claims of effectiveness, even when there is little or no supporting evidence. Worse yet are reactionary school policies, such as the perennial "get tough" approaches that are not only ineffective in the long term but also contribute to the development of systems that are hostile, aversive, socially toxic, and incompatible with optimal development of academic skills and mental health (Hyman & Perone, 1998; Skiba & Peterson, 1999).

Despite these problems and challenges, there is reason for optimism regarding our ability to positively affect the social and emotional health and resiliency of children and adolescents, even those from very adverse life circumstances. One reason for this optimism is the accumulation of a large body of scientific evidence regarding what has been termed *developmental resilience* (Doll & Lyon, 1998). This notion of resilience concerns the ability of individuals to cope successfully with adversity, risk factors, and severe life stress and for young people to develop into competent and happy adults despite these problems.

Central to this notion of developmental resilience is the idea that some characteristics of resilience—the cognitive, behavioral, and affective skills that enable one to cope effectively with adversity—may be systematically taught and learned. Although some aspects of resiliency or developmental hardiness may be innate or biologically based, the evidence convinces us that learning plays a crucial role in developing the ability to cope effectively with problems and challenges. Stated simply, the ability to be resilient and to cope effectively in the face of adverse circumstances and challenges in life is something that can be acquired in great measure through systematic and effective instruction in the critical requisite skills involved.

## SOCIAL AND EMOTIONAL LEARNING

Another reason for optimism regarding our ability to positively affect the social and emotional health and resiliency of young people is an impressive emerging body of literature in the area of SEL (Zins, Bloodworth, Weissberg, & Walberg, 2004). SEL has been defined as systematic, cohesive, and effective instructional programming designed to teach social and emotional skills to children and adolescents, to prevent mental health problems, and to provide effective early intervention for those problems that are beginning to emerge (Greenberg et al., 2003). There are many manifestations of SEL programs, ranging from simple training in social or other life skills to expansive, multipronged efforts to prevent antisocial behavior and conduct problems. Since about the early 1990s, an impressive array of evidence-based SEL programs have been developed and made available for use in education and mental health. These programs vary substantially in mode of instruction, time and resources required, target areas, and cost.

The specific type of SEL program selected will depend on the specific needs and requirements of an institution or community and the competencies and problems that are most important to target, but those efforts that are most successful tend to be implemented in a planned, cohesive manner within a system. Fragmented, uncoordinated efforts seldom produce more than superficial, short-term results (Greenberg et al., 2003).

## MODEL FOR PREVENTING BEHAVIORAL AND EMOTIONAL PROBLEMS

Educational researchers have adapted a public health prevention model for use in school systems (e.g., Merrell & Buchanan, 2006; U.S. Department of Education, 2004; Walker et al., 1996). We believe that this model (see Figure 1) has great importance for promoting SEL and for school-based promotion of children's mental health in general. Sometimes referred to as the "triangle," this model of prevention

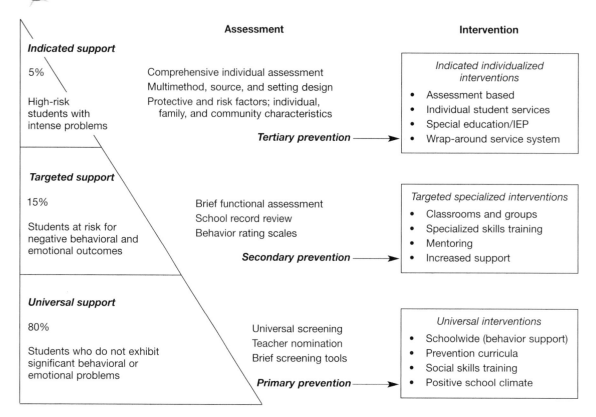

**Figure 1.** The prevention triangle model, specifically adapted for how to make systems work for assessing, identifying, and serving students with behavioral, social, and emotional problems. (*Key:* IEP, individualized education program.)

and intervention includes service delivery at three levels of prevention: students who currently are not experiencing learning or social/ behavior difficulties (*primary prevention*); students who are considered to be *at risk* for the development of learning or social/behavior difficulties (*secondary prevention*); and students who currently are experiencing significant learning or social/behavior difficulties (*tertiary prevention*).

We can visualize this model and its three levels of prevention as a triangle. The entire triangle represents all students within a school setting, the majority of whom are not experiencing difficulties (i.e., the bottom portion of the triangle), some of whom are at risk of developing significant problems (i.e., the middle portion), and an even smaller percentage who are currently experiencing significant difficulties (i.e., the top portion). Typical practice is to focus on those students who are at the top of the triangle—those who are currently experiencing significant learning or social-emotional difficulties. Practitioners tend to spend the majority of their time and effort providing tertiary prevention (i.e., individualized assessment and intervention services) to these students on a case-by-case basis. These students make up the smallest percentage of the school population, but because of the significance of their problems, they often require the majority of time and resources from school personnel (Walker et al., 1996). Figure 1 illustrates the prevention triangle model, specifically adapted for how to make systems work for assessing, identifying, and serving students with behavioral, social, and emotional problems.

Shifting to a systemwide prevention model requires looking at the "big picture" by considering the needs of *all* students, not just those who are referred because they are currently experiencing significant difficulties. The foundation of a prevention approach is the use of universal interventions (i.e., primary prevention) designed to enhance the delivery of effective instruction and improved school climate to promote the academic, social, and behavioral resilience of *all* students in the school. This idea requires that educators begin to move some resources and energy toward those children and adolescents who are not currently experiencing significant difficulties in order that they might help them acquire skills to reduce the probability that they will eventually rise to the "top of the triangle." More specifically, primary prevention for students who are not currently experiencing learning or social/behavior difficulties is accomplished through schoolwide and classwide efforts that involve the consistent use of research-based effective practices, ongoing monitoring of these practices and student outcomes, staff training, and professional development. The goal of primary prevention is to create school and classroom environments that promote student learning and health and decrease the number of students at risk for learning or social/behavior problems.

As important as it is to focus on primary prevention, we also know that not all students respond similarly to these efforts. Thus, it is important to monitor student progress and to assess whether students are at risk (i.e., in need of secondary prevention efforts) or experiencing significant difficulties (i.e., in need of tertiary prevention efforts). Identifying students at risk for learning, social-emotional, and behavior difficulties is an important aspect to comprehensive prevention efforts. For students identified as at risk and in need of secondary prevention efforts, the focus is on the delivery of specialized interventions (often at a small-group level) to prevent the worsening of problems and to prevent the development of more significant concerns. The focus on early identification and early intervention is important.

With respect to mental health and social-emotional problems of children and adolescents, we believe that this prevention model is an ideal way to think about providing SEL programs and other services. Thinking in this way about the challenges you face in promoting social-emotional wellness and mental health among children and adolescents makes these challenges more manageable. Instead of waiting until students have developed severe problems and require extensive time and effort to simply be managed, you can continually focus a portion of your resources on prevention activities that will ultimately reduce the number of students at the "top of the triangle."

## REFERENCES

Costello, E.J., & Angold, A. (2000). Developmental psychopathology and public health: Past, present, and future. *Development and Psychopathology, 12*, 599–618.

Cowen, E.L. (1994). The enhancement of psychological wellness: Challenges and opportunities. *American Journal of Community Psychology, 22*, 149–179.

Doll, B., & Lyon, M.A. (1998). Risk and resilience: Implications for the delivery of educational and mental health services in schools. *School Psychology Review, 27*, 348–363.

Farmer, E.M.Z., & Farmer, T.W. (1999). The role of schools in outcomes for youth: Implications for children's mental health services research. *Journal of Child and Family Studies, 8*, 377–396.

Greenberg, M., Domitrovich, C., & Bumbarger, B. (2001, March 30). The prevention of mental health disorders in school-age children: Current state of the field. *Prevention and Treatment, 4*, Article 1. Retrieved November 19, 2005, from http://journals.apa.org/prevention/volume4/pre0040001a.html

Greenberg, M.T., Weissberg, R.P., O'Brien, M.U., Zins, J.E., Fredericks, L., Resnick, H., et al. (2003). Enhancing school-based prevention and youth development through coordinated social, emotional, and academic learning. *American Psychologist, 58*, 466–474.

Hoagwood, K., & Erwin, H. (1997). Effectiveness of school-based mental health services for children: A 10-year research review. *Journal of Child and Family Studies, 6*, 435–451.

Hyman, I., & Perone, D. (1998). The other side of school violence: Educator policies and practices that may contribute to student misbehavior. *Journal of School Psychology, 36*, 7–27.

Merrell, K.W., & Buchanan, R.S. (2006). Intervention selection in school-based practice: Using public health models to enhance systems capacity of schools. *School Psychology Review, 35*, 167–180.

Satcher, D. (1999). *Mental health: A report of the surgeon general, 1999.* Washington, DC: U.S. Department of Health and Human Services.

Skiba, R., & Peterson, R. (1999). The dark side of zero tolerance: Can punishment lead to safe schools? *Phi Delta Kappan, 80*, 372–376, 381–382. Retrieved November 19, 2005, from http://www.pdkintl.org/kappan/kcur9910.htm

U.S. Department of Education, Office of Special Education (OSEP) Center on Positive Behavioral Interventions and Supports. (2004). *School-wide PBS.* Retrieved November 19, 2005, from http://www.pbis.org

Walker, H.M. (2001). Invited commentary on "Preventing mental disorders in school-aged children: Current state of the field." *Prevention and Treatment, 4*, Article 2. Retrieved November 19, 2005, from http://journals.apa.org/prevention/volume4/pre0040002c.html

Walker, H.M., Horner, R.H., Sugai, G., Bullis, M., et al. (1996). Integrated approaches to preventing antisocial behavior patterns among school-age children and youth. *Journal of Emotional and Behavioral Disorders, 4*, 194–209.

Zins, J.E., Bloodworth, M.R., Weissberg, R.P., & Walberg, H.J. (2004). The scientific base linking social and emotional learning to school success. In J. Zins, M. Wang, & H. Walberg (Eds.), *Building academic success and social-emotional learning: What does the research say?* New York: Teachers College Press.

# Design and Evidence

The research literature on social skills training programs, affective education curricula, and other types of mental health skill-building interventions is consistent in showing that, although these types of programs may produce important short-term gains within specific settings, it is very difficult to maintain these gains for long periods of time following the program intervention. In addition, the literature shows that there are similar difficulties in getting treatment gains, such as new skills, learned to generalize to settings other than where the skills were taught. These problems of maintenance and generalization constitute a significant challenge for SEL program developers and mental health researchers.

In developing *Strong Kids—Grades 3–5*, we specifically planned and programmed the curriculum for optimal maintenance and generalization, following best practices from the literature. Specifically, we have included suggestions and activities within each of the 12 lessons that are aimed at promoting the generalization of new skills learned across settings other than the intervention setting (e.g., home, community, other school settings) and the maintenance of these skills over time. At the end of each of the 12 lessons is a section titled "Tips for Transfer Training." This brief section includes suggested activities and methods in the following three areas, which are based on literature on effective instructional approaches for teaching social-behavioral skills authored by Sugai and colleagues (e.g., Langland, Lewis-Palmer, & Sugai, 1998; Sugai, Bullis, & Cumblad, 1997):

1. *Precorrect*—activities designed to help the group leader anticipate errors and difficulties that students may have in learning new skills, to maximize the efficacy in teaching new skills that are sequenced instructionally to previously taught skills

2. *Remind*—suggestions for providing verbal or visual prompts to students that will help remind them of steps, sequences, skills, and actions that are needed to engage effectively in new skills as they are taught

3. *Reinforce*—prompts to provide verbal praise or other forms of social reinforcement as students successfully approximate and perform the new skills they are taught in *Strong Kids—Grades 3–5*

In addition to the Tips for Transfer Training, each lesson has embedded within it suggestions for group leaders to develop and model examples of new skills and to help students see the need for these skills. These suggestions are aimed at making the lessons optimally relevant to students, thus increasing the potential effectiveness of each lesson. Homework assignments and take-home handouts are provided in several of the 12 lessons, tactics that are further designed to reinforce learning outside of the *Strong Kids—Grades 3–5* instructional setting. Finally, the optional, but highly recommended, booster lesson provides an opportunity to reteach and reemphasize critical *Strong Kids—Grades 3–5* content and skills after a period of time—usually several weeks to a few months—following completion of the 12 lessons. The booster lesson was specifically developed to help increase maintenance of gains from the curriculum over time.

We applaud the current movement toward the use of scientifically based curricula and programs in education and mental health services. SEL programs that are built on good scientific principles of instruction and behavior change and that have demonstrated evidence of effectiveness to support them are a key to making the kind of impact that we believe is necessary to help prevent and remediate the broad range of social, emotional, and mental health problems that plague our society. Several professional organizations have developed standards for determining whether or not prevention/intervention programs have sufficient evidence behind them to be considered effective from a scientific standpoint. Some of the names that have been used for programs that meet these standards include *empirically validated treatment, empirically supported treatment,* and our own preference, the more generic term, *evidence-based program.*

Since the initial development of the Strong Kids curriculum (including *Strong Start, Strong Kids—Grades 3–5, Strong Kids—Grades 6–8,* and *Strong Teens*), we have made extensive efforts to experimentally test the effectiveness of these programs. To date, several studies have been conducted on the effectiveness of various versions of the Strong Kids curriculum, under a variety of conditions. Each of these studies has found that groups of students who participated in the *Strong Kids—Grades 3–5, Strong Kids—Grades 6–8,* or *Strong Teens* programs have showed significant gains in their knowledge of curriculum concepts of SEL. Some of the studies have shown significant reductions of problem emotional-behavioral symptoms as a result of participating in the programs. In addition, some of the studies have evaluated the social validity of the programs from teacher and student perspectives. These studies, without exception, showed a very high amount of satisfaction and confidence in the programs by both students and teachers.

We encourage interested curriculum users and others to read detailed descriptions of these studies on our web site at http://strongkids.uoregon.edu. As we have already noted, our research efforts with the Strong Kids curriculum are continuing, and we hope to greatly expand the available evidence in support of this curriculum. We will post summaries and reports of research studies on the Strong Kids web site as they become available.

## REFERENCES

Langland, S., Lewis-Palmer, T., & Sugai, G. (1998). Teaching respect in the classroom: An instructional approach. *Journal of Behavioral Education, 8,* 245–262.

Sugai, G., Bullis, M., & Cumblad, C. (1997). Provide ongoing skill development and support. *Journal of Emotional and Behavioral Disorders, 5,* 55–64.

# Preparing Your Lessons and Your Students

To implement *Strong Kids—Grades 3–5*, you should have access to an overhead projector, overhead transparency film sheets, a copy machine, chart paper, and chalk or a marker board. The lessons provide templates for overhead transparencies. Although it is not essential to make overhead transparencies of these masters, we have found that doing so provides the advantage of being able to go over a graphic illustration or chart in front of the class while you introduce the critical concepts that are connected to them. Alternatively, some teachers and group leaders have found that they prefer to make paper copies of the overhead transparency masters and to provide each student with a copy of these materials rather than presenting the materials with an overhead projector. Many of the lessons also include reproducible templates for in-class handouts or worksheets for students, available on the accompanying CD-ROM.

Some teachers and group leaders have found that many of the handouts and transparency masters that are included in the curriculum make ideal posters for placement in the classroom when they are enlarged on a copy machine and posted visibly for students to see. This creative use of the curriculum tools provides an excellent visual reminder for students and will increase the opportunities for reteaching and reinforcing the main concepts of each lesson throughout the week. If you have a copy machine with enlarging capabilities, we suggest that you consider creating and displaying posters to support your teaching of the curriculum.

## SUPPLEMENTARY MATERIALS

Each *Strong Kids—Grades 3–5* lesson includes one or more sheets of related or supplementary materials, which are found at the end of the lesson and on the accompanying CD-ROM. These materials are labeled throughout the text with a "reminder" symbol. For the sake of consistency, we refer to these materials as "supplements" and have titled them that way. These supplements include overhead

13

transparency masters, in-class handouts, worksheets, and homework handouts. As you prepare for each lesson, note the supplements for that lesson and how they should be used. Prior to teaching the lesson, make copies and transparency masters as needed. These supplements are all reproducible for users of the curriculum. Although we have made suggestions regarding how to use the supplementary materials, you should feel free to adapt them to your own needs and situation. For example, you might find it useful to enlarge some of the handouts or transparency masters into posters and to place them on the wall of the classroom to reinforce or visually prompt students as they learn and practice the skills promoted in *Strong Kids—Grades 3–5*.

## PROVIDING AN AGENDA

We recommend that you make use of several media sources (e.g., blackboard, flip chart) during the course of teaching *Strong Kids—Grades 3–5*. It may be helpful to outline the lesson agenda briefly in a bullet or flow chart format before the class begins in order to establish a visual reference that you can refer to with your students. In this case, an outline of the topics included in the curriculum may be useful as well as an agenda for the individual lesson.

## STATING EXPECTED BEHAVIORS

Because of the nature of the lessons in *Strong Kids—Grades 3–5*, behavior expectations for students or group members must be very clear. Some of the units revolve around sensitive issues, and every opportunity should be taken to provide instruction and subsequent reinforcement for appropriate behavior. Students should feel free to share their beliefs and feelings on the targeted topics but must not feel pressured into revealing anything that makes them feel uncomfortable. You should state expected behaviors prior to instruction, before modeling examples, and before the practice sections of lessons. In some cases, you may need to teach and reinforce behavioral expectations more frequently than these suggested times.

As a general recommendation for promoting appropriate behavior in school and related settings, we recommend that teachers and group leaders develop and teach a few simple rules for appropriate behavior. Rules should be stated *positively*, meaning that they should tell students what is expected rather than what to avoid. For example, *respect your classmates* is a positively stated rule, whereas *no fighting* is a negatively stated rule that does not tell students what specifically they should do. Rules should be simple and appropriate to the developmental level of the children for whom they are intended. In addition, the list of rules should be kept to a minimum. Usually, no more than five general rules are needed. You will find that rules are more effective when you teach them to students and then find frequent opportunities to reinforce them through reminders, examples, and so forth.

## PLANNING FOR SMOOTH TRANSITIONS

Time is one of the most precious commodities in your classroom or center. In a brief curriculum such as *Strong Kids—Grades 3–5*, the element of time is especially critical. To make the best use of your limited time in teaching the curriculum, use your transition time wisely prior to and during the lessons. We recommend that you have all materials prepared and organized for easy distribution to students. Make sure that equipment is in working order before you start the lessons. *Explicitly state directions prior to and during transitions*. If possible, precorrect for any possible behavioral difficulties.

## PHYSICAL ARRANGEMENTS

For the lessons in this curriculum, all students must have a clear view of you, the group leader. Forward facing seats or a horseshoe shape are both appropriate. You may want to preassign students to groups of two or three because they will be required to separate into groups during the application sections in some of the lessons. This practice will not only save time but will also give you control of which students are paired. Always use movement, voice level, and voice intonation to increase the interest of your student and, consequently, increase active participation.

## ADAPTATIONS FOR UNIQUE NEEDS

In many of the lessons, you will be encouraged to create scenarios pertaining to a certain topic. To facilitate and encourage student participation, think of situations that would best reflect the interests, abilities, and level of understanding of the students in your class or group. You may choose to use current situations relevant to your classroom and school or global current events to illustrate the concepts. The situations provided in the units are to be considered examples and can be modified extensively to best fit the unique needs of your students. Making appropriate adaptations for the needs of your students will not only make the delivery of lessons go more smoothly but will also aid with generalization and maintenance of new skills.

## SUGGESTIONS FOR SUCCESS

As you teach the *Strong Kids—Grades 3–5* lessons, you will increase your likelihood of success by observing and following a few additional suggestions for successful implementation of the curriculum. We have developed these suggestions through piloting the program in numerous settings and through the feedback we have received from our associates who have used it in their schools and treatment centers.

- Be sure to give the students an *overview* of each lesson's purpose. Explain that a different topic/unit will be taught each week (or as frequently as possible), as students may come to expect a continuation of a certain topic as opposed to a new topic each lesson.

- Our experience has indicated that folders that are specifically designated for students to store their handouts, notes, and homework assignment sheets will help them to keep their materials organized and will reduce the amount of time needed by the teacher or group leader to start the weekly lessons. We suggest that you consider having all of your students keep a special *Strong Kids folder* for this purpose.

- Ensure that you sufficiently *review the topics* from prior lessons and integrate concepts when at all possible.

- Introduce or reintroduce a *behavior management technique*, such as a token economy, to reinforce prosocial behaviors during the unit. Remind students of your school and classroom rules as well as the rules associated with this curriculum.

- This curriculum involves teaching a wide range of skills in a relatively short period of time. In order to use your time most effectively, *directly teach these skills*. Place your priority on instruction, and keep discussion and activity time to a minimum.

- *Reinforce* any *Strong Kids—Grades 3–5* skills that you might observe, both within and outside the teaching setting. Make sure that parents, teachers, administrators, and other staff are aware of the skills you are instructing, as your students will require frequent feedback in several settings in order for the skills to be durable and generalized.

- *Complete at least one homework example* with the entire class or group to help them understand the assignment and be prepared to complete it.

- As a general practice, we suggest that you *do not add new students to the group once it has already started*. Particularly when the program is taught to small groups of students rather than entire classrooms, we have found that having new students join the group once it has started can be disruptive to the group process and may result in a slowing of the flow of training, as well as a reduction in the willingness of group members to participate.

- Look for opportunities to *use the Tips for Transfer Training* that are found at the end of each lesson. These suggestions have been designed to facilitate the transfer of skills learned through the program across different settings and to help students maintain what they have learned over time. Again, the three areas we have included in Tips for Transfer Training include prompts for precorrecting errors in learning the expected skills, reminding students of the concepts being learned, and reinforcing students for demonstrating the skills that have been introduced and taught in the program.

- And, of course, *practice your lessons* before implementing them!

## ADAPTATIONS FOR CULTURALLY AND LINGUISTICALLY DIVERSE LEARNERS

As our society becomes increasingly diverse, researchers and practitioners are recognizing the need to address cultural issues in curriculum development and implementation. Efforts to address cultural issues have ranged from ignoring or dismissing the need for cultural adaptations to arguing the need for culture-specific research and curricula tailored for each cultural subgroup. Between these two extreme positions has emerged a set of criteria and recommendations for making cultural adaptations to existing curricula. The cultural adaptation approach retains the core assumptions and skill domains of the existing curriculum but recommends tailoring the teaching of these concepts to the specific needs of particular groups of interest. Research supports the success of making cultural adaptations to existing social and emotional curricula for specific groups (see Munoz et al., 2002; Yu & Seligman, 2002).

We began the development of the Strong Kids curriculum with the assumption that no single curriculum could meet the learning needs of all students. By focusing on teaching a set of key ideas related to SEL and resiliency, however, we believe that the curriculum can successfully meet the needs of a wide range of students when appropriate adaptations are made. Some particular cultural variables that may require attention in curriculum adaptation processes include language, race/ethnicity, acculturation, socioeconomic status, sexual orientation, religion, gender, disability status, and nationality.

## The "Big Ideas" of *Strong Kids—Grades 3–5*

As previously noted, a successful curriculum adaptation process requires particular innovations and modifications to meet the needs of specific individuals and groups, but at the same time, these adaptations must retain the general concepts, or big ideas, on which the curriculum is based. With this notion in mind, we list the most important features of the *Strong Kids—Grades 3–5* curriculum, with the hope that these ideas will be taken into account when making any type of adaptation to the curriculum. With the underlying goal of improving SEL and resiliency in children and adolescents, these big ideas include the following:

- To prevent and reduce depression, anxiety, and other internalizing social-emotional problems in children and adolescents

- To promote awareness of moods, symptoms of depression, anxiety, and social-emotional problems of students

- To teach children and youth to understand their own and other people's feelings

- To teach children and youth to understand the link between thoughts and emotions and to learn to appropriately monitor and modulate them

- To teach children and youth to identify maladaptive thoughts and irrational beliefs that may perpetuate mental health problems and to actively strive to dispute these thoughts and beliefs, replacing them with more appropriate and adaptive ones

- To help children and youth learn to approach their challenges in life with a sense of realistic optimism

- To help children and youth learn cognitive and behavioral techniques to relax and remain calm in the face of stress

- To teach children and youth problem-solving skills and effective communication skills (e.g., listening, being assertive)

- To teach children and youth to set appropriate and realistic goals based on their own values and to monitor their behavior in order to reach these goals

## Specific Strategies for Making Cultural Adaptations

Keeping these big ideas in mind, the *Strong Kids—Grades 3–5* curriculum may be adapted to better fit the needs of diverse children. For this purpose, we propose a few guidelines for making cross-cultural adaptations. These suggestions are based on our own experiences in attempting to adapt the Strong Kids curriculum with specific cultural groups. They are also based in great measure on the premises of the American Psychological Association's Guidelines for Providers of Psychological Services to Ethnic, Linguistic, and Culturally Diverse Populations (available at http:// www.apa.org).

1. Get to know your students.

   - Ask students about their cultural identities, activities, and rituals.

   - Reflect on the dominant cultural variables in your classroom and how these aspects of culture affect the way your students behave and think.

   - Identify common success and failure experiences, problem situations, and challenging life circumstances confronted by your students.

2. Get to know your students' community.

   - Visit the families and, as appropriate, the homes of students in your class or group.

   - Identify a cultural liaison (a parent or community member who identifies as a member of the target cultural group) to help you learn more about your students' culture.

   - Ask the cultural liaison to assist with the cultural adaptation process.

3. Deliver the curriculum in a manner that your students can understand.

   - Modify the language of each lesson so that your students can easily understand the key ideas.

   - Use examples and situations that match the lives of your students (e.g., change characters' names, include extended family, include children who use wheelchairs, use problem examples that your students have experienced).

4. Encourage tolerance.

   - Teach students ways to show respect for different cultural groups.

   - Encourage and reinforce students for respecting the examples and comments made by their peers.

   - Establish and enforce a classroom rule that teasing and name-calling are not allowed.

5. Adapt assessment tools.

   - Adapt the assessment materials so that students can understand (e.g., language, context).

   - Pilot-test some of the assessment materials with small groups of students prior to implementing the curriculum to ensure that students understand the questions.

6. Become aware of variations within cultures.

- Do not assume too much about a student's culture or ethnicity.

- Avoid making overgeneralizations about cultural groups. Not all members of a culture act the same way.

- Examine your own values, assumptions, and worldviews and how these are the same and different from those of your students.

- Continually examine the accuracy and fairness of your assumptions about the beliefs and behaviors of different cultural groups.

7. Seek feedback.

- View the adaptation process as an ongoing process.

- Consult with students, your colleagues, and community members about the relevance and accuracy of the adaptation efforts.

- Ask the students how well the curriculum is matching their needs and life experiences.

In sum, adapting *Strong Kids—Grades 3–5* or any other SEL curriculum for use with culturally and linguistically diverse learners may be challenging, but it is essential if the curriculum is to have the most meaningful impact on the learners. The suggestions we have offered in this section may be useful as a guide to making the flexible *Strong Kids—Grades 3–5* program appropriate for children and youth from a variety of cultural backgrounds.

## REFERENCES

Munoz, R.F., Penilla, C., & Urizar, G. (2002, May 8). Expanding depression prevention research with children of diverse cultures. *Prevention and Treatment, 5.* Retrieved November 19, 2005, from http://www.journals.apa.org/prevention/volume5/pre0050013c.html

Yu, D.L., & Seligman, M.E.P. (2002). Preventing depressive symptoms in Chinese children. *Prevention and Treatment, 5.* Retrieved November 19, 2005, from http://www.journals.apa.org/prevention/volume5/pre0050009a.html

# Overview of the Lessons

*S*trong Kids—Grades 3–5 consists of 12 carefully sequenced lessons, designed for maximum impact on cognitive, affective, and social functioning within a relatively brief period of time. Each of these lessons is overviewed in this chapter. Read these descriptions carefully prior to preparing your first lesson so that you will understand the lesson sequencing and the big ideas behind *Strong Kids—Grades 3–5*.

## LESSON 1: ABOUT *STRONG KIDS:* EMOTIONAL STRENGTH TRAINING

In the first lesson, About *Strong Kids:* Emotional Strength Training, students are introduced to the *Strong Kids—Grades 3–5* curriculum. A general overview of the individual lessons and the overall curriculum is presented, providing students with information regarding what they can expect over the course of the instruction. Critical terms such as *emotion, self-esteem, depression,* and *anxiety* are defined for the first time, and general behavior expectations are outlined. Students are made aware of the importance of this type of curriculum so that they are able to understand why appropriate behaviors such as respect for others, confidentiality of shared information, and adequate lesson preparation are integral parts of the experience. If optional student assessments are administered as part of the curriculum, they should be given to students for completion during this first lesson.

## LESSONS 2 AND 3: UNDERSTANDING YOUR FEELINGS

The second and third lessons, Understanding Your Feelings (1 and 2), are intended to improve the emotional vocabulary, awareness, and resiliency of students. Being able to understand and recognize one's emotions is an important skill to all individuals during all stages of their lives because people experience emotions at school, at home, at work, and at play. Being able to recognize one's emotions and react in a positive way, even when the feeling is not a good one, will allow students to create and sustain positive relationships in school and throughout their lives.

In Understanding Your Feelings 1, students learn to identify different types of feelings and distinguish feelings as being comfortable and uncomfortable. They learn to recognize what situation might cause them to feel a certain way. The goal of this lesson is to apply the skills learned to different situations at different times and in different settings. In Understanding Your Feelings 2, the feelings identification skills are extended to include how one might express different feelings. Students learn that, although it is okay to have any feeling, there are appropriate and inappropriate ways of showing or expressing feelings. Given a way of expressing a feeling, students identify the way as "okay" or "not okay." Students then have the opportunity to apply their new skills in application exercises, making it more likely that they will be able to generalize the new skills to other situations.

## LESSON 4: DEALING WITH ANGER

The fourth lesson, Dealing with Anger, teaches students that everyone experiences anger in his or her life. Many students, however, are not able to appropriately understand and effectively deal with their anger. Misunderstanding anger, and an inability to appropriately manage it, can often manifest itself in inappropriate behaviors such as arguments and fights, depression, and severe frustration, each of which can have unfortunate consequences.

This lesson teaches students to understand their anger through a multistep Anger Model and teaches four skills for helping them manage their anger. Anger is introduced as one of many normal emotions that serve a purpose in helping people to understand and adapt to the world. It is important that students understand two basic concepts: 1) that anger is a normal emotion, and 2) that anger serves the important function of protection and motivation in our lives. We also seek to make an important distinction for students between anger as a normal, healthy emotion and *aggression*, a chosen behavior that is often inappropriate.

Students are taught to understand anger using the six-step, sequential Anger Model to improve their ability to recognize what anger looks like in action. In this lesson, students learn that anger does not "just happen." It is triggered by predictable events and progresses through a series of steps within which individuals can play an active role. Students are taught to understand their active roles in the anger process and the fact that they are not helpless "victims" of their anger, but are active in choosing how to respond to anger.

## LESSON 5: UNDERSTANDING OTHER PEOPLE'S FEELINGS

The purpose of the fifth lesson, Understanding Other People's Feelings, is to introduce students to the concept and practice of empathy and thus help them better understand others' feelings. Although the previous three lessons have focused on students' own feelings, Lesson 5 covers recognizing the emotions of others and sharing their perspectives, an essential skill in conflict resolution and compassion. Students who can identify the feelings of others are more likely to be tolerant of people with different views. Students will learn to see a clear link in how their actions can affect the emotions of other people.

Children with antisocial tendencies often experience what is called *hostile attribution* in which they misperceive others' emotions as anger. This misperception can lead to aggression and violence. Students who practice empathy skills are more able to see a variety of emotions other than anger. By learning to look for physical cues (called *clues* in this lesson), they may be more likely to discern the true feelings of others.

Lesson 5 first explains key concepts and then moves into identifying clues about what emotions other people are feeling. Once students are able to model the correct identification of clues, the lesson progresses to a role play in which students will experience how people may perceive the same situation differently. They will be asked to take the perspectives of others in order to gain a greater understanding of empathy. Finally, the homework handout provides opportunities for students to apply these skills to their own life experiences.

## LESSONS 6 AND 7: CLEAR THINKING

Individuals who are depressed and anxious are very likely to develop or have previously developed patterns of unrealistic, distorted, and otherwise maladaptive cognitions or thoughts. The Clear Thinking lessons, Lessons 6 and 7, are designed to help students to recognize positive and negative thought patterns and how they contribute to their moods, choices, and actions in positive and negative ways. The lesson is divided into two parts: Clear Thinking 1 and Clear Thinking 2. Clear Thinking 1 teaches students strategies helpful in recognizing negative and maladaptive thought patterns by providing descriptions of some of the more common thinking errors that individuals employ. When possible, the thought patterns such as "binocular vision," "dark glasses," and "black-and-white thinking," are depicted both as visual icons and in simplified language to facilitate comprehension and retention. Clear Thinking 2 uses the information provided in Clear Thinking 1 to teach students techniques for applying strategies to dispel negative thoughts as they occur in any common situations they may face. Practice exercises and vignettes are used for discussion.

## LESSON 8: THE POWER OF POSITIVE THINKING

Lesson 8, The Power of Positive Thinking, provides students with strategies to offset negative thought patterns that can surface as a result of any given daily interaction. For students prone to negative thinking, pessimistic feelings are redirected through exercises, examples, and situations designed to encourage a focus on the larger picture and to foster optimistic thinking. The new (broader) focus reduces the students' tendency to attribute negative events to themselves by presenting other possibilities to their perceived failures. Similarly, looking at when, where, or to whom to attribute ownership or blame also encourages students to accept credit for their successes.

The Power of Positive Thinking lesson is designed to arm all students, not just those who may be prone to pessimism and spirals of negativity, with a way to think about daily events optimistically so that reasonable attributions can be made. The method includes training students to spot the situations in which attribution can be an internal success, an external failure, or simply an opportunity to learn.

## LESSON 9: SOLVING PEOPLE PROBLEMS

The ninth lesson, Solving People Problems, is designed to promote awareness of useful strategies for resolving conflict between and among peers. Interpersonal conflict provides one of the most fertile breeding grounds for depression, anxiety, and negative thinking. Thus, learning appropriate and effective ways to resolve these conflicts may be a strong preventive factor for deterring emotional problems as well as social problems.

As conflicts may occur daily and can be a source of stress and frustration for students, step-by-step outlines for resolving conflicts are presented. This lesson details the use of a problem-solving model for managing day-to-day conflicts with peers and presents techniques for its use and application. The lesson is predominantly organized to address conflicts with peers; however, application of various strategies such as deal-making, compromising, discussion, and brainstorming are presented in situations that involve hierarchical relationships as well. Students will learn from this lesson that conflict is often a natural part of social interaction and that, with the tools to address conflict, more social interactions can be approached with confidence. Practice exercises and role-play situations are also used as examples and teaching tools.

## LESSON 10: LETTING GO OF STRESS

Using appropriate techniques to manage stress is an important strategy to promote emotional resilience and prevent physical and emotional problems. Lesson 10, Letting Go of Stress, provides the foundation for teaching students about stress and relaxation. Through the lesson and activities, the students will learn how to identify stress in their lives. An opportunity is provided for students to learn a few relaxation techniques that have been proven to be effective with many people as well as to generate their own ways of coping with stress. The homework assignment allows students to apply the discussed techniques.

Students begin to learn about themselves and how to deal with stress in an effective and healthy manner. Stress is a fact of every person's life. The sooner students learn how to identify it and deal with this aspect of being human, the better their chances are for a healthy existence. Learning how to let go of stress is an integral skill in the development of a strong and resilient kid.

## LESSON 11: BEHAVIOR CHANGE:
## SETTING GOALS AND STAYING ACTIVE

Lesson 11, Behavior Change, is subtitled Setting Goals and Staying Active. Throughout life, people are asked to achieve many goals. Frequently, they are not taught the steps that are necessary to achieve these goals. Research supports the idea that students who are able to set and achieve goals independently perform better than those students who are told what goals to achieve. This evidence also confirms that learning how to engage more consistently in appropriate positive activities can help to reduce symptoms of depression.

The six steps outlined in this lesson are all necessary in order for students to attain their goals as well as to identify their values in the different domains of their lives. Learning these steps and having immediate success by implementing them is crucial to the success of this lesson. If students set a short-term goal first and are successful in the goal-attainment process, then they will be more likely to use the process again in other applications. These steps are beneficial for students' academic achievement, and research indicates that when individuals set realistic and attainable goals they begin taking control of their lives, which leads to an increase in the amount of positive activities they engage in.

Students who are engaged in positive activities, where they contribute and feel a sense of community, are less likely to suffer from depression. Studies also indicate that a reduced level of activity can lead to low self-esteem and, in turn, hinder an individual's sense of accomplishment and worth. This lesson teaches students the skills necessary to set realistic short- and long-term goals, to identify the key steps in attaining their goals, and to apply the procedures to their own lives by increasing the amount of positive activities they are engaged in. Developing skills for increasing positive activities through setting and attaining positive goals is of critical importance in sustaining positive mental health.

## LESSON 12: FINISHING UP!

The title of the final lesson, Finishing UP!, has a double meaning. It implies that this lesson is the final one in the curriculum, but it also shows how we are striving to end on a positive or upbeat note, celebrating the accomplishments that have been made through involvement with the *Strong Kids—Grades 3–5* curriculum. This lesson provides the opportunity for students to review key points and terms from the lessons presented throughout the term. Issues of confidentiality are revisited, and information for handling more critical emotional issues (utilizing appropriate resources) is covered. The Finishing UP! lesson also provides an opportunity for teachers to assess students using follow-up measures that can be compared with the information gained from the optional preassessments that may be administered at the time the first lesson is presented.

## BOOSTER LESSON

The appendix contains a supplemental or "booster" lesson for *Strong Kids—Grades 3–5*. The idea of a booster session is to help students who have already completed *Strong Kids—Grades 3–5* to maintain the skills they have acquired and to strengthen the other positive changes that may have occurred through their participation in the curriculum. The booster activities are designed to be a review of the skills and strategies already covered in *Strong Kids—Grades 3–5*. Research on SEL interventions has indicated that the addition of a booster or review lesson several weeks to a few months following completion of the intervention may help to strengthen the skills and other positive changes that resulted from the intervention and may help maintain these positive changes over time.

This optional lesson is intended to be flexible to the needs of specific groups of students. If you prepare carefully by selecting only the most important areas that your students need extra help with, this lesson may be conducted as a single review lesson, with the flexibility allowing you to focus only on the area or areas that need the most attention. On the other hand, if you consider all of the activities and concepts within this lesson to be important review elements for your students, then this lesson may require two sessions. It is essential to balance the specific skills needs of your students with the amount of time available.

A common question we have received as we have conducted trainings for Strong Kids group leaders is "When should I use the booster lesson?" There is no simple answer to this question, and we don't intend for the booster lesson to be implemented on a specific time schedule. We recommend, however, that at least 1 month has elapsed between the completion of *Strong Kids—Grades 3–5* and the presentation of the booster lesson. We also recommend that any booster lessons are within the same school year as when the curriculum was originally taught. One recommended possibility would be to teach *Strong Kids—Grades 3–5* during the beginning of the school year (fall) and then conduct the booster session(s) in late winter or early spring. It would also be possible to spread out the booster lesson into two components, separated by a week or more.

## FINAL COMMENTS

Good luck as you prepare to use *Strong Kids—Grades 3–5*. We have field-tested this curriculum with scores of teachers and mental health professionals in the United States and elsewhere and have made many improvements to it based on their feedback from experience using it with a large number of children and in a large variety of settings. Our efforts to create an effective, user-friendly, and practical mental health promotion program, coupled with the real-world experience and feedback we gained during 5 years of research and development, have convinced us that the Strong Kids curriculum has much to offer and can be a valuable tool for facilitating SEL, promoting resilience, and teaching coping skills.

# The *Strong Kids—Grades 3–5* Curriculum

**LESSON 1**

**TEACHER NOTES**

_____

_____

_____

_____

_____

_____

_____

_____

_____

_____

_____

_____

_____

_____

_____

_____

_____

_____

_____

# About *Strong Kids*

## *Emotional Strength Training*

### Purpose

- To introduce students to the *Strong Kids* curriculum

### Objectives

- Students will identify the purpose of the *Strong Kids* curriculum.

- Students will complete the pretest assessment (optional); provide additional time if necessary.

- Students will learn the expected behaviors for participation in the program.

| MATERIALS NEEDED |
|---|

- ❑ Supplement 1.1 (overhead transparency)
- ❑ Supplement 1.2 (overhead transparency)
- ❑ Supplement 1.3 (homework handout)

For ease of use, *Strong Kids—Grades 3–5* is referred to as *Strong Kids* throughout the lessons.

**2–5 minutes**

# Introduction

Communicate the lesson's purpose and objectives clearly. Explain to your students that they will be starting a new curriculum, *Strong Kids*. Tell them how often it will be taught, and give examples of some of the topics to be covered. Let them know that the skills learned during this unit are skills that are vital to their social and emotional health and will be important during all phases of their lives.

### Sample Script

*Today, we will begin a new unit called Strong Kids. In this unit, we will discuss how to understand our emotions and the emotions of others. We will also discuss how to solve problems, how to set goals, and how to think in a way that helps us in life. We will meet [once per week] for [one class period]. You will learn important new skills that will help you work well with others and make good choices. Everyone needs to be healthy—emotionally and physically. This unit will help you learn skills that you may use to be emotionally healthy throughout your life.*

**15 minutes**

# Optional Pretest Assessments

If you wish to use any assessment tools to evaluate student growth during the *Strong Kids* curriculum, now is a good time to have your students complete the pretest portion. You can administer the assessments again after Lesson 12 to gauge student growth. You may use an assessment tool of your own choosing, or you can go the *Strong Kids* web site (http://strongkids.uoregon.edu) and use some or all of the tools we have developed for this purpose.

Pass out the pretests, and tell your students not to worry if they do not know the answers or are not familiar with the topics. Tell them that the pretest is only to test their background knowledge and measure their learning throughout the *Strong Kids* unit. When all students have a copy of the pretest, provide them with the appropriate instructions and allow them about 15 minutes to complete the assessment.

### Sample Script

*First, we are going to take a brief test that will help me to know how much you already know about emotions and feelings. It will take about 15 minutes. Do your best work, and answer all of the questions. Raise your hand if you need help reading or understanding any of the questions.*

**2–5 minutes**

# Introduction to the
# Topics Covered in the Curriculum

Using Supplement 1.1 as an overhead transparency, introduce the topics, and provide a brief explanation for each of the lessons. You may use your own words or use the sample script.

### Sample Script

*During this 12-lesson program, we will be discussing these topics. (Refer to overhead.) Today's lesson will help us to understand our goals for Strong Kids. The next two lessons will help us learn to identify our emotions and good ways to express them. The next lesson talks about our anger and also gives us good ways to deal with it. The following lesson teaches us to notice and better understand other people's feelings, while the next three lessons teach us to think in ways that help us in life. We will also learn how to solve people problems or conflicts. Finally, we will learn how to relax, keep active, and achieve our goals.*

## Awareness or Disclaimer Statement: Students with Serious Problems

Explain to your students that this unit will be focusing on life skills, but this may not be enough help for kids with serious emotional problems. Students experiencing a large amount of depression or anxiety, for example, should be identified and helped by a professional. Use the provided script or you may choose to use your own words to better suit your students.

### Sample Script

*The Strong Kids unit will be focusing on life skills and may not be enough help for students experiencing a large amount of depression or anxiety. If you feel you are experiencing these issues or you know someone that might, see me or get help from* [provide names of school counselor, psychologist, or social worker].

## Defining Behavior Expectations

Explain to your students that they may be asked to share personal information with each other as they complete each lesson. Tell them that their participation is voluntary and that they can choose to stop sharing their feelings or their story if they begin to feel uncomfortable. If students feel uncomfortable sharing in a large group, tell them that they may speak to you individually. Explain to your students that they are now a part of a group with important rules.

Use Supplement 1.2 as an overhead transparency to provide the class with examples and nonexamples of the rules. You can also ask the class to share their own examples or nonexamples.

### Sample Script

*During this unit, you may be asked to share stories about when you felt a strong emotion, such as anger, or when you've had a problem. You can raise your hand when you have a story to share. When someone is sharing a story, we will listen quietly and respectfully and remember that, because stories might be personal, they will just stay in the group. If you decide that you no longer want to share your story or if you begin to feel uncomfortable, you may stop at any time. If you do not feel comfortable sharing your story with the whole group but you feel like you want to talk to someone, please speak to me after class.*

Introduce important group/class rules for participation in *Strong Kids*.

1. Respect others.

2. Come prepared.

3. Personal things stay in the group.

### Sample Script

*You are now a part of a group with some important rules. Here are the rules:*

- **Respect others**—*Listen quietly when someone is speaking.*

- **Come prepared**—*Do homework assignments.*

- **Personal things stay in the group**—*Be respectful, and do not gossip. (For younger students, you may need to explain what gossip is, such as "saying things about other people that might hurt their feelings.")*

# Closure

Gather your students together, and review the introduction's main points.

- What are the rules of the group?

### Sample Script

*Today, we talked about Strong Kids, the new program we will be using. For the next few months, we will be learning about our feelings, learning how to deal with them, and learning other important life skills. During this time, we need to remember our three rules: 1) respect others, 2) come prepared, and 3) personal things stay in the group.*

# Homework Handout

Pass out the homework handout, Supplement 1.3, Introducing *Strong Kids*. Tell students that they are to answer the questions the best they can.

 # Strong Kids Lessons

1. About *Strong Kids:* Emotional Strength Training

2. Understanding Your Feelings 1

3. Understanding Your Feelings 2

4. Dealing with Anger

5. Understanding Other People's Feelings

6. Clear Thinking 1

7. Clear Thinking 2

8. The Power of Positive Thinking

9. Solving People Problems

10. Letting Go of Stress

11. Behavior Change: Setting Goals and Staying Active

12. Finishing UP!

# ★ STRONG KIDS™ Strong Kids Rules

1. **Respect others.**

    • Listen quietly when others speak!

2. **Come prepared.**

    • Do your homework!

3. **Personal things stay in the group.**

    • Be respectful—don't gossip!

 **Introducing Strong Kids**

Name (optional): _____

**Directions:** Think of a time when you felt really happy. Use this memory to answer the next few questions.

1.   What happened?

_____

_____

_____

2.   What thoughts did you have?

_____

_____

_____

3.   How did you know you were happy? What signs indicated this?

_____

_____

_____

4.   How did you show others you were happy?

_____

_____

_____

*Strong Kids—Grades 3–5: A Social and Emotional Learning Curriculum*
by Kenneth W. Merrell, with assistance from Dianna Carrizales, Laura Feuerborn,
Barbara A. Gueldner, and Oanh K. Tran © 2007 University of Oregon. All rights reserved.

**LESSON 2**

# Understanding Your Feelings 1

**TEACHER NOTES**

_____
_____
_____
_____
_____
_____
_____
_____
_____
_____
_____
_____
_____
_____
_____
_____
_____

## Purpose

- To teach students to identify and understand basic emotions

## Objectives

- Students will identify feelings as comfortable or uncomfortable.
- Students will generalize or apply this lesson to real-life situations.

### MATERIALS NEEDED

- ❑ Supplement 2.1 (overhead transparency)
- ❑ Supplement 2.2 (in-class handout)
- ❑ Supplement 2.3 (in-class handout)
- ❑ Supplement 2.4 (homework handout)
- ❑ Blank overhead transparency or chart paper for Feelings Identification
- ❑ Blank overhead transparency or chart paper for How Do You Feel?

### 2–5 minutes

# Review

To activate prior knowledge, review and discuss previous topics and main ideas. Obtain 3–5 adequate ideas. Discuss with students their responses to last week's homework assignment.

### Sample Script

*During our last meeting, I introduced you to the Strong Kids lessons. Raise your hand if you can tell me an important idea we learned about these lessons.*

## Ideas Discussed in Lesson 1

- What are the rules of the group?

### 2 minutes

# Introduction

Communicate the lesson's purpose and objectives clearly. Introduce the concept of identifying comfortable and uncomfortable feelings.

### Sample Script

*Today, we will learn to better identify our feelings or, as they're sometimes called, emotions. We will talk about different types of feelings and identify them as being comfortable or uncomfortable.*

### 5–10 minutes

# Name and Define Skills

## Activity A: Definitions

Use Supplement 2.1 as an overhead transparency to define the relevant terms.

### Sample Script

*An emotion is a feeling that is meant to tell you something about your situation. Being comfortable with a feeling means that we might feel good and enjoy that feeling. Being uncomfortable with a feeling means that the feeling might make us feel bad or upset, but it also might help us learn, grow, and change for the better.*

- ***Emotion/feeling**—A feeling inside that is meant to tell you something about your situation and gives you the motivation and energy to do something about it.*

- ***Comfortable**—Comfortable feelings make people feel good. They can help you have fun and enjoy life.*

- ***Uncomfortable**—Uncomfortable feelings make people feel not good or upset. They can also help people grow and change for the better. Uncomfortable feelings can help people notice and appreciate their comfortable feelings.*

## Activity B: Discussion

Ask the class discussion questions that aid in the comprehension of comfortable and uncomfortable feelings. Some possible questions include

- What are some examples of comfortable and uncomfortable feelings?
- How might you learn and grow from comfortable and uncomfortable feelings?
- How do you know if a feeling is comfortable or uncomfortable?

    In a brief discussion, convey the following main ideas to your students.

- Everyone has emotions or feelings, and it is okay to have any feeling.
- Emotions arise because of different situations.
- Emotions can be used to communicate how you feel and how others feel.
- There are different ways of showing feelings.
- Other people may not feel the same way you do about everything.
- You can do things to change how you feel and how others feel.

## Feelings Identification

**15 minutes**

Convey to students that identifying emotions is important so that we can learn to react in a positive way, even when feelings are uncomfortable.

### Sample Script

*Identifying our feelings is important because we all experience different emotions or feelings at home, school, or just playing or hanging out with other kids. If you can identify your feelings, you can react in a positive way, even if the feelings are uncomfortable.*

The following activity will help students identify feelings and label them as comfortable or uncomfortable. Students will be asked to get into small groups during Step 3.

Use a blank overhead transparency or chart paper to record the list of emotions generated from the following exercise.

1. Generate a list of emotions/feelings.
    - State a basic emotion, such as happy or sad, and explain that this is an emotion or a feeling.
    - Give a second example, using a more complex emotion such as excited or worried. Record both of the chosen emotions/feelings.
    - Ask students to generate other emotions or feelings, and write these feelings as well.

2. Identify emotions/feelings as comfortable or uncomfortable.
    - Model this skill using the emotions you provided in Step 1. As you provide these examples, mark a plus or minus next to the feeling; plus signifies feeling comfortable, and minus signifies feeling uncomfortable.

### Sample Script

*Happy is a comfortable feeling. When I feel happy, I feel good, and I am likely to smile. Sad is an uncomfortable feeling. When I feel sad, I feel bad, and I may even cry.*

- Pass out Supplement 2.2, Feelings Identification, as an in-class handout, and explain that students will mark comfortable feelings with a plus and uncomfortable feelings with a minus. Students complete the worksheet independently as an in-class handout.

3. Break into discussion groups.

- Have students break into groups of 3–5 people to discuss what they marked on their worksheets. Alternately, you can group students in pairs of two and let them use a "pair and share" approach to the activity so that each child will be sure to be heard.

- Monitor groups closely.

- Be careful to monitor your reactions to the evaluations the students produce. For example, if students identify hate or anger as comfortable emotions, do not express disappointment or dismay. Rather, use the exercise as a tool to help students increase their emotional awareness, which should ultimately prove to have numerous benefits.

4. Conduct a follow-up discussion.

- Ask students if they felt that any of the emotions were complicated to identify as comfortable or uncomfortable.

- Using examples students provide, explain that not all emotions can be easily described or labeled as comfortable or uncomfortable. For example, surprised can be both comfortable and uncomfortable, depending on the situation.

- Discuss these emotions with your students. Encourage them to pay attention to the feelings in their bodies, the expressions of their faces, and the thoughts in their minds to help them identify complicated emotions. Some complicated emotions are frustration, anxiety, guilt, and jealousy.

### Sample Script

*Sometimes it's difficult to label an emotion as comfortable or uncomfortable. For example, surprised could be a comfortable feeling if you are surprised by getting an extra present. Or surprised could be an uncomfortable feeling if you are surprised by a flat tire on your bike or a broken shoelace when you are tying your shoes.*

 10 minutes

# How Do You Feel?

Ask students to return to their large group seating arrangement, if appropriate. Convey to students the importance of understanding when you might have comfortable and uncomfortable feelings.

*Sample Script*

*Now that we know that feelings can be both comfortable and uncomfortable, we are going to talk about when you might have those feelings.*

Use a blank overhead transparency or chart paper to record examples of how you might feel at different times.

1.  Generate examples of feelings in different situations.

    - State a basic emotion, such as happy or afraid, and describe when you felt that way. Label it as a comfortable or uncomfortable feeling. You might say, "For instance, I feel afraid when I see a big spider. That is an uncomfortable feeling for me."

    - Give a second example, using a more complex emotion such as excited or worried. You might say, "I get excited when I ride a roller coaster. That is a comfortable feeling for me."

    - Ask students to generate other emotions or feelings that they have had in certain situations. Then, write the emotion or feeling only, and ask students to label the emotion as comfortable or uncomfortable. Label the emotion with a plus for comfortable and a minus for uncomfortable.

    - Pass out Supplement 2.3, How Do You Feel?, as an in-class handout. Explain that students will choose a word to write after the "I feel" part of each sentence and then use their own words to describe when they feel that way. Students complete the in-class handout independently during class. Have students mark a plus for comfortable and a minus for uncomfortable feelings. Make sure to tell students not to worry about getting it wrong because there are no right or wrong answers.

2.  Conduct a follow-up discussion.

    - Ask students to volunteer to share a response from Supplement 2.3.

    - After students volunteer a response, ask them to state whether the example was a comfortable or uncomfortable feeling or situation for them.

    - Ask students how they knew that feeling was comfortable or uncomfortable.

    - Ask students how they can differentiate among emotions.

2–5 minutes

# Closure

Gather your students together, and review the lesson's main points.

- What are emotions or feelings?
- How do you identify comfortable and uncomfortable feelings?
- Emotions are sometimes difficult to identify.

*Sample Script*

*Everyone has emotions or feelings. Today, we learned how to identify different types of emotions or feelings. We talked about feelings as being comfortable or uncomfortable and talked about times when we feel different types of emotions.*

# Homework Handout

Pass out the homework handout, Supplement 2.4, About My Feelings, and explain the instructions. Students are asked to complete sentences describing their feelings.

# Tips for Transfer Training

### Precorrect

Tell your students to try to identify the feelings they experience throughout the day (particularly a day that includes plenty of emotional activities, e.g., field trips, assemblies, testing days). Once they identify or label the feeling they are experiencing, they should investigate whether the feelings are comfortable or uncomfortable.

### Remind

If you notice students having difficulty expressing themselves in words (getting frustrated and showing it by rolling their eyes, feeling tired or upset and expressing it by putting their heads on their desks), remind them to tell you what they are feeling using the words or emotional labels learned in this lesson.

### Reinforce

Praise your students (or give them a small reward if you have a behavior management system in your class) if you notice any of your students expressing an emotion or expressing that their emotion is comfortable or uncomfortable ("That homework was hard. I felt frustrated when that homework was hard," or "I felt bad when Sally called me a name.").

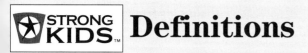 **Definitions**

## Emotion/feeling

A feeling inside that is meant to tell you something about your situation and gives you the motivation and energy to do something about it

## Comfortable

Comfortable feelings make people feel good. They can help you have fun and enjoy life.

## Uncomfortable

Uncomfortable feelings make people feel not good. They can also help people grow and change for the better. Uncomfortable feelings can help people notice and appreciate their comfortable feelings.

*Strong Kids—Grades 3–5: A Social and Emotional Learning Curriculum*
by Kenneth W. Merrell, with assistance from Dianna Carrizales, Laura Feuerborn,
Barbara A. Gueldner, and Oanh K. Tran © 2007 University of Oregon. All rights reserved.                    43

# ⭐ STRONG KIDS™ Feelings Identification

**Directions:** This activity will help you learn to identify comfortable and uncomfortable feelings. Pick one of the lists on this worksheet. Put a plus (+) next to any words that you think describe comfortable feelings, and put a minus (–) next to any words that you think describe uncomfortable feelings.

## Comfortable feelings

- Make people feel good
- Can help you have fun and enjoy life

## Uncomfortable feelings

- Make people feel bad
- Can also help people grow and change for the better
- Can help people notice and appreciate their comfortable feelings

### Feeling List 1

| | | | |
|---|---|---|---|
| happy | lonely | scared | bored |
| angry | sad | upset | surprised |
| strong | proud | afraid | glad |
| shy | worried | tired | love |

### Feeling List 2

| | | | |
|---|---|---|---|
| lonely | sorry | guilty | worried |
| happy | miserable | excited | proud |
| confused | strong | scared | loyal |
| crabby | surprised | upset | bored |
| serene | inspired | warm | angry |
| anxious | frustrated | thrilled | furious |
| compassion | ignored | embarrassed | love |

# STRONG KIDS™ **How Do You Feel?**

**Directions:** From the list of feelings at the bottom of this sheet, choose words to write after the "I feel" part of each sentence, and then use your own words to describe when you feel that way.

I feel _____ when _____ .

I feel _____ when _____ .

I feel _____ when _____ .

I feel _____ when _____ .

I feel _____ when _____ .

I feel _____ when _____ .

I feel _____ when _____ .

I feel _____ when _____ .

## Feeling List

| | | | |
|---|---|---|---|
| happy | bored | joyful | thrilled |
| lonely | angry | thankful | safe |
| excited | proud | stupid | worried |
| scared | tense | hyper | upset |

*Strong Kids—Grades 3–5: A Social and Emotional Learning Curriculum*
by Kenneth W. Merrell, with assistance from Dianna Carrizales, Laura Feuerborn,
Barbara A. Gueldner, and Oanh K. Tran © 2007 University of Oregon. All rights reserved.

# ★ STRONG KIDS™  About My Feelings

Name (optional): _____

**Directions:** Complete each of these sentences about feelings in your own words, using real examples about how you feel.

I am afraid when _____.

I am really good at _____.

I get excited when _____.

Most of the time I feel _____.

I am happy when _____.

I feel upset when _____.

I am sad when _____.

I am calm when _____.

I get really mad when _____.

I am thankful for _____.

I am lonely when _____.

I feel proud when _____.

I am ashamed of _____.

I am disappointed when _____.

I hope that _____.

*Strong Kids—Grades 3–5: A Social and Emotional Learning Curriculum*
by Kenneth W. Merrell, with assistance from Dianna Carrizales, Laura Feuerborn,
Barbara A. Gueldner, and Oanh K. Tran © 2007 University of Oregon. All rights reserved.

**LESSON 3**

**TEACHER NOTES**

# Understanding Your Feelings 2

## Purpose

- To teach students appropriate ways of expressing feelings

## Objectives

- Students will be able to distinguish between positive and negative examples of expressing feelings.

- Students will generalize or apply this lesson to real-life situations.

**MATERIALS NEEDED:**

- ❏ Supplement 3.1 (overhead transparency)
- ❏ Supplement 3.2 (overhead transparency)
- ❏ Supplement 3.3 (in-class handout)
- ❏ Supplement 3.4 (overhead transparency)
- ❏ Supplement 3.5 (homework handout)

## 2–5 minutes    Review

To activate prior knowledge, review and discuss previous topics and main ideas. Obtain 3–5 adequate ideas. Discuss with students their responses to last week's homework assignment.

### Sample Script

*During our last meeting, we learned to identify our feelings. Raise your hand if you can tell me an important idea we learned in our last class.*

### Ideas Discussed in Lesson 2

- What are emotions or feelings?
- How do you identify comfortable and uncomfortable feelings?
- Emotions are sometimes difficult to identify.

## 2 minutes    Introduction

Communicate the lesson's purpose and objectives clearly. Students will learn appropriate ways of expressing feelings.

### Sample Script

*In today's lesson, we will talk about ways of expressing feelings. There are positive, or appropriate, ways of expressing feelings and there are negative, or inappropriate, ways of expressing feelings. If we are able to identify our feelings in certain situations, we can react more positively.*

## 5 minutes    Identify Actions that Follow Feelings

### Activity A

Convey the following main ideas to your students using your own words or the following statements.

- Everyone has emotions or feelings, and it is okay to have any feeling.
- Emotions arise because of different situations.
- Emotions can be used to communicate how I feel and how others feel.
- There are different ways of showing feelings.
- Other people may not feel the same way I do about everything.

### Activity B

Identify common actions associated with an emotion. Use examples such as frustrated or happy, or use your own example or an emotion solicited from the students.

*Sample Script*

*Today, we are going to talk about the things that we do when we have certain feelings. For example, frustration is an uncomfortable feeling. When we feel frustrated, we usually feel like giving up, stopping what we are doing, walking away, or getting angry. Happy is a comfortable feeling. When we feel happy, we usually feel like we can do things well, we smile more, and we feel good inside.*

Take a few moments to discuss with the class appropriate and inappropriate ways to express opinions and ideas in different situations. Use the examples used previously for this discussion (e.g., frustration, happiness). Use the following guideline:

- Inappropriate expression can hurt yourself or others.

- Appropriate expression is a form of sharing ideas that is more respectful, while minimizing the chances of hurting someone.

# Positive and Negative Examples of Showing Feelings

Use Supplement 3.1, Ways of Showing Feelings 1, as an overhead transparency to teach appropriate ways of expressing feelings. Provide opportunities for response or ongoing assessment by randomly selecting students to respond.

Use the prompt, "Is this example an appropriate way of showing feelings or is it NOT an appropriate way of showing feelings?" Mark a smiley face on the overhead next to the example to indicate that this is an appropriate or okay way of expressing your emotions. Mark a frowning face to indicate that this is NOT an appropriate way of expressing your emotions.

## Examples and Nonexamples from Supplement 3.1

Read the first two examples, and provide the correct answer for each by stating whether the reaction is okay or not okay.

### Situation 1 (Example)

*The student feels angry, stops, counts to 10, and then feels calm. This is an appropriate way of showing feelings because the student used a strategy to think about his response before acting on his emotion. His reaction did not hurt the student or others.*

### Situation 2 (Nonexample)

*The student feels angry and yells at the person next to her. This is NOT an appropriate way of showing feelings because the student reacted to her emotion without thinking first. She was hurting her friend.*

Read the third example, and ask students to respond to the question.

### Situation 3 (Example)

*The student feels angry, takes a deep breath, and walks away from the upsetting situation. Is this an appropriate way of showing feelings or NOT an appropriate way of showing feelings?*

Continue marking the response with the appropriate symbol.

### Situation 4 (Nonexample)

*The student feels mad, takes a deep breath, and then bangs his fist on his desk, hurting his hand.*

### Situation 5 (Nonexample)

*Once the student is aware that she is angry, she refuses to talk to any of her friends.*

### Situation 6 (Example)

*The student realizes she is feeling angry, calms down, and talks to the teacher about what made her angry.*

Using Supplement 3.2, Ways of Showing Feelings 2, as an overhead transparency, continue with the exercise by asking students to generate one appropriate way of showing feelings for a chosen emotion and one inappropriate way of showing the same chosen emotion. Think of more complex emotions like proud or sorry as you suggest feelings to work on.

**12 minutes**

# Practice Situations and Application

Photocopy or print out Supplement 3.3, Practice Situations, and cut out the individual situations. If you wish, use your own practice situations written on strips of paper or index cards.

Group the students in groups of 4–5 people to complete the application exercise. Give each group one situation. Explain to students that they must do the following:

1. Read aloud the situation.

2. Identify the emotion they would probably have if they were in the given situation.

3. Identify the emotion as comfortable or uncomfortable.

4. Generate at least three positive examples of expressing that emotion.

Use Supplement 3.4, Practice Application, as an overhead transparency for students to view during this group exercise.

After the exercise, keep students in their small groups but come together as a large group for discussion. Ask a volunteer from each group to read the group's situation aloud. Ask students to give their group's responses to these questions. Make time to ask volunteers to role-play how they would respond to the situations described.

*Situation 1*

*You find out that one of your classmates has been saying things that are not true about you.*

*Situation 2*

*Everyone in your class except you has been invited to a classmate's birthday party.*

*Situation 3*

*You are the goalkeeper for your soccer team. During the last 2 minutes of the game, a ball slips by you, and the other team scores to win the game.*

*Situation 4*

*You let a friend borrow your favorite CD. Your friend took forever to return it, and when you played the CD, you realized your friend must have scratched it because it now skips on tracks 3 and 4.*

*Situation 5*

*You don't want your mom or dad to see your report card because of some poor grades you received.*

*Situation 6*

*You are getting ready to go on a trip for which you have been waiting a long time. You find out that the weather is bad and your parents might cancel the trip.*

# Closure

Gather your students together, and review the lesson's main points.

- How do you identify appropriate and inappropriate ways of expressing emotions?
- What are positive ways of showing emotions?
- How do you identify your own feelings for certain situations?

### Sample Script

*Identifying our emotions is important because we all experience different emotions or feelings at home, school, and just hanging out. If you can identify your feelings, you can react in a positive way even if the feelings are uncomfortable. Everyone has emotions or feelings.*

# Homework Handout

Pass out the homework handout, Supplement 3.5, Reacting to Emotional Situations. Go over the directions with students, and answer any questions they may have. Remind students that there are no right or wrong answers to the questions. Everyone experiences each situation differently.

# Tips for Transfer Training

## Precorrect

Tell your students to remember the last two lessons and use "okay" ways of expressing their emotions during potentially emotional times of the day, such as recess period, lunch, or physical education.

## Remind

Similar to Lesson 2, if you notice students having difficulty expressing their emotions (getting bored and showing it by an outburst, e.g., "This is boring! I hate this!"; feeling upset at another peer and expressing this by yelling at him or her), remind them that these are NOT okay ways to express their emotions, and ask them to try expressing their emotions again in an okay way.

## Reinforce

Reward your students for displaying okay ways of expressing their emotions. Some examples of okay ways include students using "I feel" statements, talking (not yelling) out their issues with one another, or asking for help if they are getting frustrated.

# Ways of Showing Feelings 1

😊 This is an okay way to show feelings.

🙁 This is NOT an okay way to show feelings.

____ 1. The student feels angry, stops, counts to 10, and then feels calm.

____ 2. The student feels angry and yells at the person next to her.

____ 3. The student feels angry, takes a deep breath, and walks away from the upsetting situation.

____ 4. The student feels mad, takes a deep breath, and then bangs his fist on his desk, hurting his hand.

____ 5. Once the student is aware that she is angry, she refuses to talk to any of her friends.

____ 6. The student realizes she is feeling angry, calms down, and talks to the teacher about what made her angry.

*Strong Kids—Grades 3–5: A Social and Emotional Learning Curriculum*
by Kenneth W. Merrell, with assistance from Dianna Carrizales, Laura Feuerborn,
Barbara A. Gueldner, and Oanh K. Tran © 2007 University of Oregon. All rights reserved.

 **Ways of Showing Feelings 2**

🙂 This is an okay way to show feelings.

🙁 This is NOT an okay way to show feelings.

**Emotion/feeling** _____

🙂 1. _____

_____

🙁 2. _____

_____

**Emotion/feeling** _____

🙂 1. _____

_____

🙁 2. _____

_____

# Practice Situations

## Situation 1

You find out that one of your classmates has been saying things that are untrue about you.

## Situation 2

Everyone in your class except you has been invited to a classmate's birthday party.

## Situation 3

You are the goalkeeper for your soccer team. During the last 2 minutes of the game, a ball slips by you, and the other team scores to win the game.

## Situation 4

You let a friend borrow your favorite CD. Your friend took forever to return it, and when you played the CD, you realized your friend must have scratched it because it now skips on tracks 3 and 4.

## Situation 5

You don't want your mom or dad to see your report card, because of some poor grades you received.

## Situation 6

You are getting ready to go on a trip for which you have been waiting a long time. You find out that the weather is bad and your parents might cancel the trip.

55

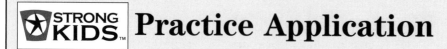

# Practice Application

**Directions:** In your group, discuss the situation, and answer the following questions.

1.  How would you feel if this happened to you?

    _____

    _____

    _____

    _____

2.  Is the feeling comfortable or uncomfortable?

    _____

    _____

    _____

    _____

3.  Name at least three okay or appropriate ways of showing how you might feel.

    _____

    _____

    _____

    _____

 **STRONG KIDS™**

# Reacting to Emotional Situations

Name (optional): _____

**Directions:** For each situation, describe the feeling you would probably have if it happened to you. Put a check in the appropriate box to show if it is a comfortable or uncomfortable feeling. Also, think about "why" you think you might feel that way. There are no right or wrong answers. Everyone experiences situations differently.

| Situation | Feeling | Comfortable | Uncomfortable |
|---|---|---|---|
| You are invited by three different students to sit with them in the cafeteria. | | | |
| One of your friends doesn't want to spend time with you anymore. | | | |
| You can't think of anything to do. | | | |
| You get picked last to play on a team. | | | |
| You are asked to do extra chores. | | | |
| You get picked first to play on a team. | | | |
| Your teacher says, "Great job. You got 100% right!" | | | |
| Your teacher says, "Your work is too sloppy. Do it over again." | | | |
| A student says, "I don't understand how to do this. Will you help me?" | | | |
| Your parents are having an argument. | | | |
| You don't have enough money to get something you want. | | | |
| Your mom or dad says, "You're too young. Wait until you're older." | | | |
| A family member is very ill. | | | |

**LESSON 4**

# Dealing with Anger

_____

_____

_____

_____

_____

_____

_____

_____

_____

_____

_____

_____

_____

_____

_____

_____

_____

## ✦ Purpose

- To teach students to understand anger and manage aggression

## ✦ Objectives

- Students will accurately list and describe the steps of the Anger Model.
- Students will be able to name and describe the anger control skills taught.
- Students will apply the Anger Model and anger control skills to situations.
- Students will generalize or apply this lesson to real-life situations.

### MATERIALS NEEDED

- ❏ Supplement 4.1 (overhead transparency and in-class handout)
- ❏ Supplement 4.2 (overhead transparency)
- ❏ Supplement 4.3, Option A (overhead transparency)
- ❏ Supplement 4.3, Option B (overhead transparency)
- ❏ Supplement 4.4 (overhead transparency and in-class handout)
- ❏ Supplement 4.5 (in-class handout)
- ❏ Supplement 4.6 (homework handout)

**2–3 minutes**

# Review

*Note:* This lesson has a lot of information and examples. It is important that you adhere to the minimum time limit allotted for each section as this lesson has many components and will require you to teach at an efficient pace. If necessary, Practice and Application can be omitted. If you find it difficult to get through the important information on dealing with anger in one lesson, you may consider dividing this lesson into two sessions.

To activate prior knowledge, review and discuss previous topics and main ideas. Obtain 3–5 adequate ideas. Discuss with students their responses to last week's homework assignment.

### Sample Script

*Recently, we learned about comfortable and uncomfortable emotions. Can anyone give me an example of a comfortable and an uncomfortable emotion? During our last meeting, we also discussed identifying and expressing our emotions. Raise your hand if you can tell me another important idea we learned in our last lesson.*

## Ideas Discussed in Lesson 3

- How do you identify appropriate and inappropriate ways of expressing emotions?
- What are positive ways of showing emotions?
- How do you identify your own feelings for certain situations?

**2–3 minutes**

# Introduction

Communicate the lesson's purpose and objectives clearly. Introduce concepts of appropriate and inappropriate ways of expressing anger and ways to cope with anger.

### Sample Script

*Today, we will talk about a feeling called anger. Anger is a normal feeling that everyone experiences. We will learn what anger looks like and what causes it. We will also learn several skills to help us deal with our anger so that we don't need to behave in a way that is inappropriate or that will hurt ourselves or others.*

**8–10 minutes**

# Name and Define Anger and Aggression

### Activity A

Use Supplement 4.1 as an overhead transparency and as a reference handout for your students. Choose students to read the definitions. Facilitate brief discussions on each item.

*Sample Script*

*Here are some important ideas that we will be discussing.*

- ***Emotion/feeling**—A feeling that comes from something happening to you that is meant to tell you something about your situation. An emotion is usually identified by feelings in your body or thoughts in your mind.*

- ***Anger**—A powerful emotion of unhappiness and dislike toward someone or something when you feel threatened or harmed.*

- ***Frustration**—A feeling of disappointment or feeling overwhelmed when something doesn't go your way or you do not get what you want.*

- ***Aggression**—Using hurtful words or inappropriate physical behaviors toward others, such as hitting, screaming, kicking, slamming doors, ignoring somebody, or giving them the silent treatment.*

- ***Anger management**—Choosing appropriate behaviors when you are angry.*

## Activity B

Convey the following main ideas to your students using your own words or the sample script.

- *All people have emotions.* Emotions are tools that help us understand and cope with a person or situation (just as our eyes and ears help us perceive the world).

- *Anger is a natural and necessary emotion.* Anger signals us to take notice and respond to a situation. Without anger, we would be limited in our ability to understand and cope (i.e., protect ourselves) with people and situations (just as without our eyes and ears we would be limited in our ability to understand the world).

- *Aggression is one of many behaviors we can choose from* to cope with situations and people when we are angry.

- *Aggression is not the best way to deal with our anger* and often leads to harmful results. There are usually better ways to deal with our anger.

*Sample Script*

*We all have eyes and ears that help us see what is around us, such as when we walk down the street or ride our bike. Feelings are like eyes and ears that help us understand our situation and deal with our problems. Anger is a strong feeling that helps us protect ourselves when someone does something that makes us mad or something happens that we don't like. For example, it is natural to become angry when someone steals from you or calls you names or to get mad because your parents grounded you for something that was unfair. However, hitting someone, yelling at someone, crying to get your way, or slamming doors isn't the best way to deal with your anger. There are other ways of dealing with it and solving the problem.*

Ask students for examples of when they have become angry and what made them angry.

### *Sample Script*

*Raise your hand if you have an example of a time when you were angry, and describe what it was that made you angry.*

## Activity C

Explain that anger can be useful, but it doesn't have to lead to aggression or frustration. There are others ways of reacting to our anger.

### *Sample Script*

*When you are angry and you yell at somebody, hit somebody, or even give somebody the "silent treatment," it does not solve the problem. Those things are inappropriate and can lead to more problems. Better or more appropriate ways of reacting to your anger include talking about your anger, problem-solving, or taking a break.*

Ask students to talk about some ways they handle their anger or frustration.

### *Sample Script*

*Raise your hand to describe ways you've used to handle your anger.*

## Activity D

Explain that anger is a normal, healthy emotion, but using aggression leads to problems.

### *Sample Script*

*Understanding our anger and dealing with it in a good way is a very important skill that we all need throughout our lives. Anger is a normal, healthy emotion that all of us will feel many times in our lives. Being angry at someone or over something is not wrong, but dealing with anger through aggression or mean behavior usually leads to more problems.*

Ask students for examples of situations when they have seen aggressive or inappropriate behaviors (e.g., hitting, yelling, having a tantrum, ignoring) used in response to feeling angry or have done these things themselves.

### *Sample Script*

*Raise your hand to describe when you've used aggressive or inappropriate behaviors to deal with anger or seen others do this.*

## Activity E

Describe short- and long-term problems for being angry and aggressive.

### *Sample Script*

*People who are often angry and aggressive can have problems making and keeping friends, doing well in school, getting along with their family, being involved in activities, and feeling happy. Even though being aggressive can get you what you want right away, it usually causes you to have many more problems later.*

| 2–3 minutes |
| --- |

# Introduce the Anger Model and Definitions

Use Supplement 4.2 as an overhead transparency to define the Anger Model. Briefly discuss each item and the definitions.

- *Trigger*—any situation that results in you feeling angry
- *Interpretation/understanding*—the process of thinking about what has happened to you and deciding what it means
- *Emotional reaction (anger)*—what you feel after interpreting a situation or trigger
- *Decision*—making a choice about the action you will take
- *Behavior*—acting out the decision that you made
- *Consequence*—the direct results of your behavior

| 10 minutes |
| --- |

# Integrate and Illustrate the Anger Model

## Activity A

Use Supplement 4.3 as an overhead transparency. Two options, A and B, are provided to give you a range of examples to choose from. Have students volunteer to read each step of the Anger Model and the corresponding script that illustrates each step. (Option A is provided here. If you choose Option B, refer to Supplement 4.3, Option B, at the end of this lesson or on the accompanying CD-ROM.)

| Steps of the Anger Model | Script for situation |
| --- | --- |
| 1. Trigger | Two days ago, you were really struggling with a problem that you felt you could not talk to anybody about because you were afraid others might find out. Your best friend convinced you to talk about it and promised to keep it secret. You just overheard two people talking about your problem. |
| 2. Interpretation | You begin wondering how they found out and who told them. As you think about it, you realize that the only person you told was your best friend. |
| 3. Emotional reaction | As you realize that your best friend must have told others, a bad feeling comes over you. You feel betrayed by your best friend. As you think about what will happen to your reputation now that your secret is known, you become furious. |
| 4. Decision | In the heat of the moment, you decide you have to do something about this now. You are so angry that you decide you are going to yell at and beat up your friend. |
| 5. Behavior | You see your best friend in the hall. You run toward your friend, yell at him or her, and push him or her into the wall. |
| 6. Consequence | You and your friend are both suspended from school for fighting and your best friend becomes your enemy. |

## Activity B

After reviewing each step in the Anger Model and the corresponding script on page 63, discuss with the class the following main points.

- A *trigger* is any situation that results in your feeling angry. It could be someone doing something to you that results in your feeling angry, you yourself doing something that results in your feeling angry, or certain life situations that result in your feeling angry.

- *Interpretation* is an automatic and active process that is based on a number of factors including past experiences, situational circumstances, and mood. When the student overheard two people talking about a problem that he or she thought was a secret, the student could have automatically begun to think about the meaning of it. The student could have interpreted the event in one of two ways: 1) the best friend disclosed the secret to other people or 2) other people already knew about the problem.

- The student's interpretation will determine his or her *emotional reaction* (e.g., anger, indifference, fear), which will in turn influence the student's decision-making process in selecting a behavioral response.

- A student's behavioral response to his or her anger is the product of a *decision*. This decision often occurs so quickly that students are unaware that they are making a decision; however, it is important that students recognize that they do make a decision in how to respond to their anger.

- A student's *behavior* produces both short- and long-term consequences. Many of these consequences are obvious (e.g., disciplinary referral, getting what you want) but many are less obvious (e.g., peer rejection, poor student–teacher relationships). It is important that students be aware of the consequences of their behaviors.

# Introduce Anger Control Skills

Use Supplement 4.4 as an overhead transparency to introduce skills used to cope with anger.

### Sample Script

*Here are several examples of things that you can do to help you deal with your anger. Although you can use all of these skills any time you are angry, they work best when you use them in the right stage of the Anger Model. First, we will describe each skill. Then, we will talk about when it is best to use that skill and apply that skill to an example.*

Briefly go through each example with your students.

- *Counting backwards* means that you quietly count backwards from 10. It is best used when you first notice that you are angry (Emotional Reaction stage). It gives you time to think about the situation and what you are going to do and calms you down.

- *If-then statements* mean that you ask yourself what might happen if you do something. They are best used when you are deciding what to do about a situation or problem (Decision stage). If-then statements help you make better choices by helping you understand the consequences of your actions.

- *Self-talk* means that you say to yourself the things that a good friend would say to calm you down, such as, "Calm down," "Take it easy," or "Let it go." It is best used when you first notice that you are angry (Emotional Reaction stage). Its purpose is to help calm you down.

- *Self-evaluation* means that you think about what you want to get out of the situation and how best to get it. It is best used when you are deciding what to do about a situation or problem (Decision stage). Its purpose is to help you get what you want out of a situation.

# Application of Anger Control Skills

Use Supplement 4.5 as an in-class handout to demonstrate the next activity. Using your own example or the suggested example, illustrate the appropriate use of the Anger Model. Read the negative example, and explicitly state that students are not using the anger control skills.

### Negative Example

*You are standing in the lunch line when someone comes up to a person in front of you and begins talking to him. As the line moves forward, the person slips into the line ahead of you and continues to talk* (Trigger). *You wonder if the person is just talking to a friend and will leave or if he is being sneaky and deliberately cutting in line. You determine that he is cutting in line* (Interpretation) *and become angry* (Emotional Reaction). *You think about what you should do and decide to yell at him* (Decision). *You step out of the line, approach him, and tell him, "No cutting, Idiot! Go to the end of the line!"* (Behavior). *He yells back, and heated words are exchanged. You shove him, and the two of you get into a shoving match. Because of this, you are both sent to the principal's office and have to stay after school for 5 days. You also have to miss a cool field trip later that week* (Consequences).

Ask the following discussion questions:

- How did this turn out?

- What went wrong?

After discussing the negative example, discuss the positive example using the anger control skills.

### Sample Script

*Now, we will repeat the situation and this time include the anger control skills that we learned. I will model the appropriate use of the anger control skills for you.*

### Positive Example

*You are standing in the lunch line when someone comes up to a person in front of you and begins talking to him. As the line moves forward, the person slips into the line ahead of you and continues to talk* (Trigger). *You wonder if the person is just talking to a friend and will leave or if he is being sneaky and deliberately cutting in line. You determine that he is cutting in line* (Interpretation) *and become angry* (Emotional Reaction). *To calm down, you quietly count backwards from 10* (Count Backwards). *After counting backwards you tell yourself, "Calm down; take it easy"* (Self-Talk). *You think about what you should do. You come up with several options and ask yourself what will happen if you do each of them* (If-Then Statements). *Next, you ask yourself what you want to get out of the situation and pick the option that will get you what you want* (Self-Evaluation). *You decide to say something but want to avoid a fight* (Decision). *You calmly approach the student and ask, "Are you in line or just talking to your friend?" He responds, "I am doing both." You say, "That's not fair for those of us who have been waiting in line. I think that you should go to the back of the line." He apologizes and goes to the back of the line* (Consequences).

Ask the following discussion questions:

- What if the student had refused?
- How did this turn out?
- Why did it turn out this way?
- What was different from the last example?

## **10 minutes** **Practice and Application**

### **Student Role Plays**

Present students with one or two situations you have developed or have students develop their own. Instruct students to label their situations using the Anger Model.

Use Supplement 4.2 as an overhead transparency for students to reference the steps in the Anger Model.

Pass out Supplement 4.4 as an in-class handout for students to reference anger control skills they can use. Have students discuss what anger control skills they would use in their example.

Then, put students in groups of 2 or 3, and ask them to role-play a positive example using the anger control skills.

### **Discussion**

After students have completed the role plays, select one of the groups' examples for discussion. Have the students present their example labeled with the steps of the Anger Model. Ask the following discussion questions:

- How did this turn out?
- Why did it turn out this way?
- What skills did you use?

## **2–3 minutes** **Closure**

Gather your students together, and review the lesson's main points.

- How do you define *emotion, anger, aggression, frustration,* and *anger management?*

- All people have emotions.
- Anger is a necessary and natural reaction.
- Aggression is not the best way to deal with anger.
- There are other ways to react to anger.
- What are the long-term problems to being angry and aggressive?
- What are the steps of the Anger Model?
- What are anger control skills?

### Sample Script

*Today, we learned about a six-step Anger Model, which included the steps: 1) trigger, 2) interpretation, 3) emotional reaction, 4) decision, 5) behavior, and 6) consequence. We also learned four useful skills for dealing with our anger. The skills included 1) count backwards, 2) if-then statements, 3) self-talk, and 4) self-evaluation.*

## Homework Handout

Pass out the homework handout, Supplement 4.6, Anger Management Worksheet, and explain the instructions. Students are to describe a recent event where someone was angry and apply that situation to the Anger Model. Then, discuss anger control skills that could be used. Students may find it useful to use Supplement 4.4 when doing this assignment.

## Tips for Transfer Training

### Precorrect

Tell your students to use their anger control skills (count backwards, if-then statements, self-talk, and self-evaluation) if they feel as if they are getting angry. Recess, lunch, and physical education periods are particularly good for this lesson's precorrection.

### Remind

If you find students who are not dealing with their anger properly, ask them whether or not they *interpreted* their *emotional reaction* and made the best *decision*. Remind them of the *consequences* for their reactions, and prompt them to use the anger control skills.

### Reinforce

If you happen to see your students using any anger control skills or providing evidence that they used the steps of the Anger Model appropriately, give them praise or reinforcement. For example, students could be rewarded for talking out their conflicts or reacting calmly to an aversive situation (an anger trigger).

# Definitions

### Emotion/feeling

A feeling that comes from something happening to you that is meant to tell you something about your situation. An emotion is usually identified by feelings in your body or thoughts in your mind.

### Anger

A powerful emotion of extreme unhappiness and dislike toward someone or something when you feel threatened or harmed

### Frustration

A feeling of disappointment or feeling overwhelmed when something doesn't go your way or you do not get what you want

### Aggression

Using hurtful words or inappropriate physical behaviors toward others, such as hitting, screaming, kicking, slamming doors, ignoring somebody, or giving them the silent treatment

### Anger management

Choosing appropriate behaviors when you are angry

 **Definitions of the Anger Model**

## Trigger

Any situation that results in you feeling angry

## Interpretation

The process of thinking about what has happened to you and deciding what it means

## Emotional reaction (anger)

What you feel after interpreting a situation or trigger

## Decision

Making a choice about the action you will take

## Behavior

Acting out the decision that you made

## Consequence

The direct results of your behavior

69

 **The Anger Model (Negative Example)**

### Trigger

Two days ago, you were really struggling with a problem that you felt you could not talk to anybody about because you were afraid others might find out. Your best friend convinced you to talk about it and promised to keep it secret. You just overheard two people talking about your problem.

### Interpretation

You begin wondering how they found out and who told them. As you think about it, you realize that the only person you told was your best friend.

### Emotional reaction (anger)

As you realize that your best friend must have told others, a bad feeling comes over you. You feel betrayed by your best friend. As you think about what will happen to your reputation now that your secret is known, you become furious.

### Decision

In the heat of the moment, you decide you have to do something about this now. You are so angry that you decide you are going to yell at and beat up your friend.

### Behavior

You see your best friend in the hall. You run toward your friend, yell at him or her, and push him or her into the wall.

### Consequence

You and your friend are both suspended from school for fighting and your best friend becomes your enemy.

*Strong Kids—Grades 3–5: A Social and Emotional Learning Curriculum*
by Kenneth W. Merrell, with assistance from Dianna Carrizales, Laura Feuerborn,
Barbara A. Gueldner, and Oanh K. Tran © 2007 University of Oregon. All rights reserved.

STRONG KID

LESSON

 **STRONG KIDS** **The Anger Model (Negative Example)**

## Trigger

You are standing in the lunch line when someone comes up to a person in front of you and begins talking to him. As the line moves forward, the person slips into the line ahead of you and continues to talk.

## Interpretation

You wonder if the person is just talking to a friend and will leave or if he is being sneaky and deliberately cutting in line. You determine that he is cutting in line.

## Emotional reaction (anger)

You become angry.

## Decision

You think about what you should do and decide to yell at him.

## Behavior

You step out of the line, approach him, and tell him, "No cutting, Idiot! Go to the end of the line!"

## Consequence

He yells back, and angry words are said. You shove him, and the two of you get into a shoving match. Because of this, you are both sent to the principal's office and have to stay after school for 5 days. You also have to miss a cool field trip later that week.

 **Anger Control Skills**

| Skill | Description | When to use |
|---|---|---|
| Count backwards | Quietly count backwards from 10 | When you first notice that you are angry *(emotional reaction)* |
| If-then statements | As you are deciding what to do, ask yourself, "If I do [blank], then what will happen to me?" | When you are deciding what to do *(decision)* |
| Self-talk | Tell yourself, "Calm down," "Take it easy," "Ignore it," or "Let it go." | When you notice that you are angry, to calm yourself down *(emotional reaction)* |
| Self-evaluation | Decide what you want to get out of the situation and how best to get it. | When deciding what you want to accomplish in the situation and what the best way is to do this *(decision)* |

STRONG KID

LESSON

 **Negative and Positive Examples**

## Negative Example

You are standing in the lunch line when someone comes up to a person in front of you and begins talking to him. As the line moves forward, the person slips into the line ahead of you and continues to talk *(trigger).* You wonder if the person is just talking to a friend and will leave or if he is being sneaky and deliberately cutting in line. You determine that he is cutting in line *(interpretation)* and become angry *(emotional re-action).* You think about what you should do and decide to yell at him *(decision).* You step out of the line, approach him, and tell him, "No cutting, Idiot!  Go to the end of the line!" *(behavior).* He yells back, and heated words are exchanged. You shove him, and the two of you get into a shoving match. Because of this, you are both sent to the principal's office and have to stay after school for 5 days. You also have to miss a cool field trip later that week *(consequences).*

## Positive Example

You are standing in the lunch line when someone comes up to a person in front of you and begins talking to him. As the line moves forward, the person slips into the line ahead of you and continues to talk *(trigger).* You wonder if the person is just talking to a friend and will leave or if he is being sneaky and deliberately cutting in line. You determine that he is cutting in line *(interpretation)* and become angry *(emotional re-action).* To calm down, you quietly count backwards from 10 *(count backwards).* After counting backwards, you tell yourself, "Calm down. Take it easy" *(self-talk).* You think about what you should do. You come up with several options and ask yourself what will happen if you do each of them *(if-then statement).* Next, you ask yourself what you want to get out of the situation and pick the option that will get you what you want *(self-evaluation).* You decide to say something but want to avoid a fight *(decision).* You calmly approach the student and ask, "Are you in line or just talking to your friend?" He responds, "I am doing both." You say, "That's not fair for those of us who have been waiting in line. I think that you should go to the back of the line." He apologizes and goes to the back of the line *(consequences).*

*Strong Kids—Grades 3–5: A Social and Emotional Learning Curriculum*
by Kenneth W. Merrell, with assistance from Dianna Carrizales, Laura Feuerborn,
Barbara A. Gueldner, and Oanh K. Tran © 2007 University of Oregon. All rights reserved.                73

# Anger Management Worksheet

Name (optional): _____

**Directions:** Describe a recent situation that you might have witnessed or been a part of that involved someone becoming angry. Be sure to include each step of the Anger Model in your description.

Trigger _____

_____

Interpretation _____

_____

Emotional reaction _____

_____

Decision _____

_____

Behavior _____

_____

Consequence _____

_____

**Directions:** Using the anger control skills you have learned, indicate the skills that could have been used in the situation you described and discuss how it could have been used. (Use Supplement 4.4 as a guide for identifying skills you can use.)

_____

_____

_____

_____

LESSON
**5**

TEACHER
NOTES

# Understanding Other People's Feelings

## Purpose

- To teach students how to identify others' emotions and to take different perspectives

## Objectives

- Students will learn to use physical cues to understand how someone else is feeling.
- Students will learn how to take the perspective of others.
- Students will generalize or apply this lesson to real-life situations.

| MATERIALS NEEDED |
| --- |

- ❏  Supplement 5.1 (overhead transparency)
- ❏  Supplement 5.2 (overhead transparency)
- ❏  Supplement 5.3 (in-class handout)
- ❏  Supplement 5.4 (homework handout)

**2–3 minutes**

# Review

To activate prior knowledge, review and discuss previous topics and main ideas. Obtain 3–5 adequate ideas. Discuss with students their responses to last week's homework assignment.

### Sample Script

*During our last meeting, we talked about inappropriate and appropriate ways to deal with your anger. Raise your hand if you can tell me an important idea we learned from this lesson.*

## Ideas Discussed in Lesson 4

- How do you define *emotion, anger, aggression, frustration,* and *anger management?*
- All people have emotions.
- Anger is a necessary and natural reaction.
- Aggression is not the best way to deal with anger.
- There are other ways to react to anger.
- What are the long-term problems to being angry and aggressive?
- What are the steps of the Anger Model?
- What are anger control skills?

 **2 minutes**

# Introduction

Communicate the lesson's purpose and objectives clearly. Introduce the concept of empathy, to understand and better identify other people's emotions.

### Sample Script

*Today, we will learn about a skill called empathy. We will learn how to notice other people's feelings, try to understand other people's feelings better, and see a situation from another person's perspective.*

 **5–8 minutes**

# Name and Define Skills

## Activity A

Use Supplement 5.1 as an overhead transparency to discuss the following terms. Choose students to read each definition. Facilitate brief discussions on each item.

### Sample Script

*Here are some important ideas that we will be discussing.*

- ***Emotion/feeling**—A feeling that comes from something happening to you that is meant to tell you something. An emotion is usually identified by feelings in your body or thoughts in your mind.*

- *Empathy*—*Understanding another person's feelings or emotions.*
- *Perspective/point of view*—*Feelings and opinions each person has in an experience.*
- *Clues/cues*—*Signals or signs you can see that tell you something about another person.*

## Activity B

Convey the following main ideas to your students using your own words or the sample script. Emphasize to students that looking for clues will help us in empathizing with others' feelings.

- The first part of empathy is finding out how someone feels.
- We can ask a person how he or she feels.
- It might be possible to tell someone's emotional state by looking for visual cues.
- People may or may not share the same perspective in the same situation.
- If we know how someone is feeling, we can better understand him or her and be empathetic.

### Sample Script

*The first part of empathy is finding out how someone else is feeling. We can ask the person how he or she feels, but first we can try to figure out how the person feels by looking for clues or cues. If we can find clues, we might be able to guess how someone is feeling. Then, we can try to see things from the other person's perspective. Different people might feel different things and feelings, even in the same situation. If we can find the other person's perspective, we might be able to understand and get along with him or her better.*

**10–15 minutes**

# Modeling Emotions

This activity is designed to give students experience in showing how a particular event can bring about an emotion, which, in turn, can be discerned by visual cues.

Use Supplement 5.2 as an overhead transparency. Without telling the students the emotion you are depicting, model "embarrassed" body language by putting your head down, your hand up to your face, and your arms close to your body. Ask students to guess the emotion that you are modeling.

### Sample Script

*I am thinking of an emotion on the overhead transparency, and I will act it out for you without telling you what it is. Pay attention to physical cues that might tell you what emotion I am feeling. Think of what emotion it is and what might have happened to me to make me feel this way.*

*Yes, I am feeling embarrassed because I fell down in front of a group of people. Now, who would like to volunteer to show an emotion? This time, try to guess what they are feeling and why they might feel that way.*

Then, have individual students choose an emotion without telling their classmates and have them model body language that reflects that emotion. Have the students guess the emotion that is being modeled. Reiterate that not everyone experiences or shows emotions the same way.

Emotions listed on Supplement 5.2 and their corresponding body language:

- *Happy*—smile, open arms, stand up straight, walk with head high, laugh

- *Sad*—put head down, pull arms close to body, shuffle feet, cry

- *Angry*—puff up lips, frown, clench fists, get red in the face (if possible!), bare teeth, cross arms, take up space (e.g., hold arms away from body), walk quickly, shake, make threatening eye contact

- *Scared*—drop head, open eyes, walk backwards slowly, tremble

- *Embarrassed*—turn head away, hunch shoulders, blush, avoid eye contact

Use as many examples as necessary for students to master identifying visual cues. Students may disagree on the emotions they feel for the same experience. This is an excellent point to discuss how people may feel differently depending on their perspective. This will be covered more in the role-play practice in Practice and Application. Probe the class for knowledge of emotions and cues that might help them discern someone else's feelings.

**2 minutes**

# Integrate Key Concepts

This section can be taught separately or woven in throughout your lesson via the example situations, modeling situation, or the student role-play situations. Begin with a discussion linking emotional cues to perspective.

### Sample Script

*Now that we know some cues to look for, we can try to figure out what someone else is going through just by looking at him or her. When have there been times in your lives when you could tell how someone else was feeling? How did you know? Were you able to take their perspective and empathize with them?*

Obtain the following main ideas from your students:

- Students can use cues to understand each others' emotions.

- Students can use this information to better understand one another.

**15 minutes**

# Practice and Application

This exercise is designed to have students role-play situations, identify physical cues of others, and understand someone else's perspective.

## Activity A

Using the example provided or your own example, engage in the following activity as an introduction to Activity B, a classwide activity. Act out the following situation (use physical cues, such as frowning, irritated voice, disappointed words, or annoyed look to demonstrate the physical cues that go with emotions).

### Example

*You are Emma. Today is Thursday. You come into the classroom excited about the class field trip that you have been waiting for all year. Your teacher tells the class that the field trip has been cancelled, but you will get to watch an educational video instead. Along with the video there will be an assignment due for Monday. Now, you have homework over the weekend.*

Discuss the following questions with the class:

- What do you think (name of person) is feeling?

- What physical cues lead you to that conclusion?

- Whose perspective could you also consider? Why?

- What would that perspective be?

- Why is it important to know someone else's perspective?

## Activity B

Use Supplement 5.3 as an in-class handout. Photocopy the handout page, and cut out each situation.

Have students get into four groups. Give each group one situation, and ask the group members to read the situation. Once the groups have read their situations, have them nominate two people to act as the characters in the situation. Have the two nominated people act out the situation for their group. Then, have the students respond to the situation using the questions listed with each situation. Have students think about the following for each situation:

- What do you think (person) is thinking and feeling?

- What physical cues lead you to that conclusion?

- Whose perspective could you also consider? Why?

- What would that perspective be?

- Why is it important to know someone else's perspective?

Have the groups exchange situations so that they can practice each of the four situations.

### Situation 1

*You are Maylee. Today is Friday, and you're upset. You were supposed to go to your friend's house over the weekend, but instead you have to work on a school project. You would have the whole weekend to play at your friend's house if you didn't have that project due on Monday. You know your parents will make you work on your project and won't let you go to your friend's house. If only that project wasn't due on Monday, then you could go to your friend's house, and that would make you so happy!*

### Situation 2

*You are Jason. A new student, Juanita, started school today and has been assigned to your class. You said "hello" to her, but she didn't say anything back and walked away. You also noticed that when other students try to talk to her, she doesn't say anything either. When the teacher introduces her to the class, the teacher says that she just moved here from a different country.*

### Situation 3

*You are Tamika. During recess, you are playing on the swings alone, like you usually do. Two of the popular girls come up to you and tell you to get off the swings because they are going to play on them. You look around and don't know what to do. You get off the swings and walk a little ways away and watch. You feel like you're going to cry but try not to because the kids are looking at you.*

### Situation 4

*You are Lakota. You are working with José on a social studies project. The teacher told you to make a poster for your project. You have some great ideas about how to do the poster but noticed that José is already starting on it. You really want your ideas to be included in the poster, but José doesn't seem to listen to your ideas. José just told you that your ideas are boring.*

## 2–3 minutes Closure

Gather your students together, and review the lesson's main points.

- How do you define *emotion, empathy, perspective,* and *cues?*
- What visual cues can you look for to tell someone's emotional state?
- People can have different perspectives in a similar situation.
- People may feel different emotions in a similar situation.
- People can use information about others' feelings to be empathetic toward them.

 (*Tip:* Ask students to model various emotions from Supplement 5.2 as a group when you call them out).

### Sample Script

*Today, we talked about empathy. We discussed some ways to recognize other people's feelings and how to take their perspective. See if you can use the skills you learned today to better understand your friends and family and to find their perspectives. When you are not sure how someone is feeling, see if you can use cues to understand him or her. Using those cues, you can try to take their perspective.*

# Homework Handout

Pass out the homework handout, Supplement 5.4, Empathy Assignment. Students are asked to respond to questions about times when they could tell how someone was feeling, the cues they noticed, and what they did to help that person. They are asked to think of ways they could understand the feelings of someone who they know is having a hard time right now.

# Tips for Transfer Training

## Precorrect

Prior to social situations, both occasional and routine, remind your students to use visual clues and change their perspective to try to understand the other person's point of view. Situations like physical education, recess, pep assemblies, school dances, and competitive athletic and academic events may be particularly good times to use this precorrection.

## Remind

If you notice a student is not using his or her empathy skills, remind the student to try to understand how the other person is feeling. The student should use physical or visual cues to try to see the situation as the other person would. This reminder may be particularly useful during confrontations.

## Reinforce

If you notice your students using any of the skills related to empathy, give them praise or other types of reinforcement. Remember to specify your reinforcements by naming the particular skill you observed. For example, a reinforcement given to a student for comforting another may resemble the following statement: "Jason, I noticed you used your empathy skills to understand how Jim may be feeling. Very good!"

 **Definitions**

### Emotion/feeling

A feeling that comes from something happening to you that is meant to tell you something. An emotion is usually identified by feelings in your body or thoughts in your mind.

### Empathy

Understanding another person's feelings or emotions

### Perspective/point of view

Feelings and opinions each person has in an experience

### Clues/cues

Signals or signs you can see that tell you something about another person

 **Emotions**

## Happy

Smile, open arms, stand up straight, walk with head high, laugh

## Sad

Put head down, pull arms close to body, shuffle feet, cry

## Angry

Puff up lips, frown, clench fists, get red in the face, bare teeth, cross arms, take up space (e.g., hold arms away from body), walk quickly, shake, make threatening eye contact

## Scared

Drop head, open eyes, walk backwards slowly, tremble

## Embarrassed

Turn head away, hunch shoulders, blush, avoid eye contact

83

 ## Small-Group Student Role Plays

### Situation 1

You are Maylee. Today is Friday, and you're upset. You were supposed to go to your friend's house over the weekend, but instead you have to work on a school project. You would have the whole weekend to play at your friend's house if you didn't have that project due on Monday. You know your parents will make you work on your project and won't let you go to your friend's house. If only that project wasn't due on Monday, then you could go to your friend's house, and that would make you so happy!

- What do you think Maylee is thinking and feeling?

- What physical cues lead you to that conclusion?

- Whose perspective could you also consider? Why?

- What would that perspective be?

- Why is it important to know someone else's perspective?

### Situation 2

You are Jason. A new student, Juanita, started school today and has been assigned to your class. You said "hello" to her, but she didn't say anything back and walked away. You also noticed that when other students try to talk to her, she doesn't say anything either. When the teacher introduces her to the class, the teacher says that she just moved here from a different country.

- What do you think Juanita is thinking and feeling?

- What physical cues lead you to that conclusion?

- Whose perspective could you also consider? Why?

- What would that perspective be?

- Why is it important to know someone else's perspective?

*continued*

*Strong Kids—Grades 3–5: A Social and Emotional Learning Curriculum*
by Kenneth W. Merrell, with assistance from Dianna Carrizales, Laura Feuerborn,
Barbara A. Gueldner, and Oanh K. Tran © 2007 University of Oregon. All rights reserved.

STRONG KID
LESSON

## Situation 3

You are Tamika. During recess, you are playing on the swings alone, like you usually do. Two of the popular girls come up to you and tell you to get off the swings because they are going to play on them. You look around and don't know what to do. You get off the swings and walk a little ways away and watch. You feel like you're going to cry but try not to because the kids are looking at you.

- What do you think Tamika is thinking and feeling?
- What physical cues lead you to that conclusion?
- Whose perspective could you also consider? Why?
- What would that perspective be?
- Why is it important to know someone else's perspective?

## Situation 4

You are Lakota. You are working with José on a social studies project. The teacher told you to make a poster for your project. You have some great ideas about how to do the poster but noticed that José is already starting on it. You really want your ideas to be included in the poster, but José doesn't seem to listen to your ideas. José just told you that your ideas are boring.

- What do you think Lakota is thinking and feeling?
- What physical cues lead you to that conclusion?
- Whose perspective could you also consider? Why?
- What would that perspective be?
- Why is it important to know someone else's perspective?

*Strong Kids—Grades 3–5: A Social and Emotional Learning Curriculum*
by Kenneth W. Merrell, with assistance from Dianna Carrizales, Laura Feuerborn,
Barbara A. Gueldner, and Oanh K. Tran © 2007 University of Oregon. All rights reserved.

 **Empathy Assignment**

Name (optional): _____

Think of two times when you could tell how someone else was feeling.

1. _____

   _____

2. _____

   _____

How could you tell?  (What were the cues that you noticed)?

1. _____

   _____

2. _____

   _____

What did you do, or what could you do to help that person?

1. _____

   _____

2. _____

   _____

Think of someone who you think might be having a hard time now. Think of some ways you can understand this person's feelings using the skills you have learned in this lesson.

1. _____

   _____

2. _____

   _____

*Strong Kids—Grades 3–5: A Social and Emotional Learning Curriculum*
by Kenneth W. Merrell, with assistance from Dianna Carrizales, Laura Feuerborn,
Barbara A. Gueldner, and Oanh K. Tran © 2007 University of Oregon. All rights reserved.

## LESSON 6

# Clear Thinking 1

**TEACHER NOTES**

## ⭐ Purpose

- To identify negative thought patterns and to develop an awareness of the range of emotions

## ⭐ Objectives

- Students will have an increased awareness of the range of their emotions.
- Students will learn that identifying negative thought patterns can help create a healthy lifestyle.
- Students will learn to identify common thinking errors.
- Students will apply their knowledge of negative thought patterns and thinking errors to real-life situations.

| MATERIALS NEEDED |
| --- |
| ❑ Supplement 6.1 (overhead transparency) |
| ❑ Supplement 6.2 (overhead transparency and in-class handout) |
| ❑ Supplement 6.3 (overhead transparency) |
| ❑ Supplement 6.4 (overhead transparency and homework handout) |

**2–3 minutes**

# Review

To activate prior knowledge, review and discuss previous topics and main ideas. Obtain 3–5 adequate ideas. Discuss with students their responses to last week's homework assignment.

*Sample Script*

*During our last meeting, we talked about how to recognize and understand other people's emotions. Raise your hand if you can tell me an important idea we learned in our last class.*

## Ideas Discussed in Lesson 5

- How do you define *emotion, empathy, perspective,* and *cues?*
- What visual cues can you look for to tell someone's emotional state?
- People can have different perspectives in a similar situation.
- People may feel different emotions in a similar situation.
- People can use information about others' feelings to be empathetic toward them.

**2–3 minutes**

# Introduction

Communicate the lesson's purpose and objectives clearly. Introduce the concept of emotions and their varying levels of intensity. Students will learn to identify negative thoughts and thinking errors.

*Sample Script*

*Today, we will continue to discuss emotions. We will see that emotions can be experienced in different degrees of intensity: some low, some medium, and some high. This is a lot like measuring the temperature outside with the thermometer: sometimes it's cold, sometimes it's warm, and sometimes it's really hot. We will learn to identify when our thoughts and feelings are low, medium, and high. Sometimes these thoughts and feelings can be negative and inaccurate about the situation. In the next lesson, we'll learn ways to change these negative thoughts to create a healthy lifestyle.*

**25 minutes**

# Identify Intensity of Emotions, Negative Thoughts, and Common Thinking Errors

## Activity A

Use Supplement 6.1 as an overhead transparency. Model an example of feeling angry, and discuss where your emotions were on the thermometer. Then, ask several students to volunteer to identify certain situations they may have experienced that involved emotions such as anger, sadness, and fear. Have the students select the appropriate level, or "temperature," of emotional intensity for that situation.

*Sample Script*

*I'm going to ask a volunteer to think of a time he or she felt angry and use the picture of the thermometer to help explain to the rest of the class the level of emotion he or she felt in that situation. If you felt a little angry, you might point to one of the bottom lines in the "low" area. If you felt a lot angry, you might point to one of the top lines in the "high" area; to show something in between, you can point to one of the lines in the middle in the "medium" area. For example, I felt [insert emotion] when [insert a situation] happened the other day. I was at the [insert level from thermometer] point on the thermometer. Would anyone like to share an anger experience with the class?*

## Activity B

Tell the students that thoughts often go along with emotions and feelings and that it is important to pay attention to both our thoughts and feelings. Make the point that their thoughts and emotions happen at about the same time and that it is very important to think about our thoughts when we're feeling strong emotions.

*Sample Script*

*When we feel strong emotions, we have thoughts that go with those emotions that happen at about the same time. It's important to pay attention to both our feelings and our thoughts.*

Ask the students who shared their feelings or emotions in Activity A to talk about what their thoughts were while they were experiencing the feeling or emotion.

*Sample Script*

*Remember the feelings you talked about with the thermometer? What were the thoughts that you had that went along with those feelings?*

## Activity C

Use Supplement 6.2 as an overhead transparency and in-class handout to explain the activity. For this activity, you will describe the different types of common thinking errors. Provide the students with the handout to illustrate the six types of thinking errors.

*Sample Script*

*Now that we have talked about how our emotions can come in different degrees and that there are thoughts that come with those emotions, we will move on. It is important to understand that sometimes when our emotions are very strong, we can make a mistake or a thinking error about a situation. In other words, the thought we are having may not be completely accurate. For example, when we make a mistake we might blame others for what happened and not take responsibility for our behaviors. If we identify these thinking errors, we can change the way we look and react to a situation. We will discuss six of the most common thinking errors that people make.*

Use the overhead transparency to guide a thorough explanation of each of the six thinking errors. Explain that people could experience no thinking errors, one thinking error, or multiple thinking errors for one situation. Provide students with the opportunity to ask questions about the types of thinking errors.

## Activity D

Use Supplement 6.3 as an overhead transparency to discuss the six situations, and ask the students to identify which thinking errors are being demonstrated by referring to their handout of thinking errors (Supplement 6.2). Reveal only one situation at a time to illustrate each thinking error. Read each situation aloud, and encourage students to follow along on the overhead.

After reading each situation, ask, "Which of the six thinking errors is occurring in this story?"

Call on individual students to identify the thinking error that is occurring. Provide feedback as needed if a student provides an incorrect answer. Use this exercise as an opportunity to motivate students to apply the information from the lesson and to get them thinking. Be prepared for students attributing several thinking errors for each situation. If this occurs, help students to discriminate amongst the thinking errors, explaining how they are different. The bold phrases in each example will help you appropriately identify the thinking error.

### Situation 1 (Making it personal)

*Michael's parents are getting a divorce. He thinks that **this is all his fault** because he has been getting into trouble lately.*

### Situation 2 (Fortune-telling)

*Marcella's teacher suggested that she run for class president. She decided not to run because **she knew no one would vote for her.***

### Situation 3 (Binocular vision)

*Farah got a bad grade on her spelling test. Now she thinks that **she is the worst student in the class.***

### Situation 4 (Dark glasses)

*Ahmad's soccer coach gave him a lot of praise and encouragement in soccer practice. As Ahmad was leaving practice, the coach mentioned that Ahmad should practice his dribbling skills at home. Ahmad was upset about **how poorly he played at practice.***

### Situation 5 (Black-and-white thinking)

*Ling was grounded for not doing her chores. She thought to herself, "I am **always** the bad kid. My sister Kimmy is **always** the good kid."*

### Situation 6 (Blame game)

*Latisha got in trouble from her parents for taking grape juice into the living room. Her brother bumped into her, and the grape juice spilled all over the floor and stained the carpet. Her parents told her she had to clean it up because they had told her not to take the grape juice out of the kitchen. Latisha **felt that her brother should be the one to clean it up.***

**2–5 minutes**

# Closure

Gather your students together, and review the lesson's main points.

- Identifying negative thought patterns can create a healthy lifestyle.

- What are some common thinking errors?

- How do you apply negative thought patterns and thinking errors to your own life?

### Sample Script

*Today, we discussed the range of our emotions. We learned how to identify common thinking errors. In the next lesson, we'll learn how to change these thinking errors to help create a healthy lifestyle. The homework will help you apply what you've learned today about negative thought patterns and thinking errors to your own lives.*

**10 minutes**

# Homework Handout

Use Supplement 6.4 as an overhead transparency and homework handout. Explain that students will be asked to list four situations where they had a negative thought or saw someone experiencing a negative thought pattern on a television show. The exercise asks them to identify their feelings, level of feelings, whether the feelings were comfortable or uncomfortable, their thoughts, and what type of thinking error was made. When explaining the assignment, you may choose to provide a personal example of a time you experienced a negative thought and engaged in a thinking error or use a well-known television or movie character. You can fill out the parts of the chart as you model the use of the chart.

### Sample Script

*On this homework handout, you'll be asked to list four situations where you had a negative thought or saw someone on TV having a negative thought. You're going to identify the kind of thinking error you or the person might have made. I'll start with an example.*

(*Important*: Have the students work through *at least one example* on the homework sheet before the session ends so that they will have something to work on for the next lesson, as it will be a continuation of this activity. At the end of the lesson, instruct the class to bring their completed homework to the next class.)

### Sample Script

*It is very important that you bring your completed homework assignment to our next meeting. We will be using your examples for the next lesson.*

Be sure to prepare for the possibility that most students may not remember to complete the homework or bring completed exercises to the next lesson.

# Tips for Transfer Training

## Precorrect

Tell your students to use their knowledge of Clear Thinking to identify the opportunities to refute negative thinking throughout the day. Situations like report-card day or results to state and classroom assessments may be particularly good times to use this precorrection.

## Remind

If you notice students using one of the six types of negative thinking, ask them if they recognize what type of thinking they are using, and strategize effective ways to reframe the events and/or to examine the evidence that supports or refutes their thinking.

## Reinforce

Reward students observed identifying positive thinking opportunities. Catch and compliment students identifying and using evidence-based steps to reframe negative thinking.

# Feelings Thermometer

High

Medium

Low

 # Common Thinking Errors

**Binocular vision**
Looking at things in a way that makes them seem bigger or smaller than they really are

**Black-and-white thinking**
Looking at things in only extreme or opposite ways (for example, thinking of things as being good or bad, never or always, all or none)

**Dark glasses**
Thinking about only the negative parts of things

**Fortune-telling**
Making predictions about what will happen in the future without enough evidence

**Making it personal**
Blaming yourself for things that are not your fault

**Blame game**
Blaming others for things you should take responsibility for

# Situations

1. Michael's parents are getting a divorce. He thinks that **this is all his fault** because he has been getting into trouble lately.

2. Marcella's teacher suggested that she run for class president. She decided not to run because **she knew that no one would vote for her.**

3. Farah got a bad grade on her spelling test. Now she thinks that **she is the worst student in the class.**

4. Ahmad's soccer coach gave him a lot of praise and encouragement in soccer practice. As Ahmad was leaving practice, the coach mentioned that Ahmad should practice his dribbling skills at home. Ahmad was upset about **how poorly he played at practice.**

5. Ling was grounded for not doing her chores. She thought to herself, "I am **always** the bad kid. My sister Kimmy is **always** the good kid."

6. Latisha got in trouble from her parents for taking grape juice into the living room. Her brother bumped into her, and the grape juice spilled all over the floor and stained the carpet. Her parents told her she had to clean it up because they had told her not to take the grape juice out of the kitchen. Latisha **felt that her brother should be the one to clean it up.**

95

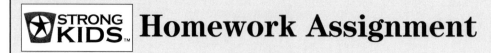

# Homework Assignment

Name (optional): _____

***Directions:*** List four situations where you had a negative thought. For each negative thought, write what you were feeling, where on the thermometer your emotion was, if that emotion was comfortable or uncomfortable, what the negative thought was, and what type of thinking error you made. You can also use situations you saw on television of someone experiencing a negative thought pattern. Answer the same questions for what the person experienced.

| Situation | What were you (or the person) feeling? | Where on the thermometer was your (or the person's) emotion? | Was that comfortable or uncomfortable? | What was your (or the person's) negative thought? | What type of thinking error did you (or the person) make? |
|---|---|---|---|---|---|
| 1. | | | | | |
| 2. | | | | | |
| 3. | | | | | |
| 4. | | | | | |

*Strong Kids—Grades 3–5: A Social and Emotional Learning Curriculum*
by Kenneth W. Merrell, with assistance from Dianna Carrizales, Laura Feuerborn,
Barbara A. Gueldner, and Oanh K. Tran © 2007 University of Oregon. All rights reserved.

## LESSON 7

# Clear Thinking 2

**TEACHER NOTES**

_____
_____
_____
_____
_____
_____
_____
_____
_____
_____
_____
_____
_____
_____
_____
_____
_____
_____
_____
_____

## Purpose

- To provide students with relevant and applicable skills for refuting negative thought patterns

## Objectives

- Students will learn specific skills designed to refute negative thought patterns.

- Students will learn skills to discriminate harmful and pervasive negative thought patterns from acceptable (evidence-based) negative thoughts.

- Students will practice refuting negative thoughts in situations representing real-life problems.

| MATERIALS NEEDED |
| --- |

- ❑ Supplement 7.1 (overhead transparency)
- ❑ Supplement 7.2 (overhead transparency)
- ❑ Supplement 7.3 (overhead transparency)
- ❑ Supplement 7.4 (overhead transparency)
- ❑ Supplement 7.5 (overhead transparency)
- ❑ Supplement 7.6 (homework handout)

# Review

To activate prior knowledge, review and discuss previous topics and main ideas. Obtain 3–5 adequate ideas.

### Sample Script

*During our last meeting, we talked about ways to identify negative thoughts and how to recognize the thinking errors that can lead to negative thoughts. We spent a lot of time talking about six thinking errors and discussed an example of each thinking error.*

## Ideas Discussed in Lesson 6

- Identifying negative thought patterns can create a healthy lifestyle.

- What are some common thinking errors?

- How do you apply negative thought patterns and thinking errors to your own life?

## Review of Thinking Errors

The previous lesson's homework assignment will be used in Looking for Evidence and Learning to Reframe Negative Thoughts, Activity C, for discussion and group activity.

Use Supplement 7.1 as an overhead transparency. (This transparency was also part of last week's lesson.) Tell the students that they are going to review the thinking errors and then move on to the "next level" where they start to change negative thought patterns.

### Sample Script

*I am going to show you those thinking errors again because, in today's lesson, we are moving into the "next level," where we will start thinking of ways to change those negative thoughts if ever we should have them.*

Review the six negative thinking errors. Use questions like "What was another one?" or "What can you tell me about this one?" Expose one image at a time, providing hints and feedback.

The thinking errors are as follows:

- *Binocular vision*—looking at things in a way that makes them seem bigger or smaller than they really are (Example: You're invited to a beach party. It will be lots of fun, but you don't know how to swim or don't want to have to wear a bathing suit, and that is all you can think of.)

- *Black-and-white thinking*—looking at things in only extreme or opposite ways (e.g., thinking of things as being good or bad, never or always, all or none, friend or enemy) (Example: If my friend can't come to my birthday party, then she must not like me. There is no other explanation.)

- *Dark glasses*—thinking about only the negative parts of things (Example: I messed up on a major school project, so now my whole day is ruined.)

- *Fortune-telling*—making predictions about what will happen in the future without enough evidence (Example: Natalie is not going to like the present I got for her.)

- *Making it personal*—blaming yourself for things that are not your fault (Example: If I had stopped the dog and played with it, he wouldn't have been hit by the bicycle.)

- *Blame game*—blaming others for things that you should take responsibility for (Example: You blame the teacher for a bad grade when you didn't study for the test.)

 **2–5 minutes**

# Introduction

Communicate the lesson's purpose and objectives clearly. Introduce the concept of changing thinking errors to positive or more realistic thoughts.

### Sample Script

*We spent some time reviewing the six kinds of thinking errors. We will now learn to change those thinking errors to positive or more realistic thoughts.*

**20 minutes**

# Looking for Evidence and Learning How to Reframe Negative Thoughts

Use the following sample script or your own words to describe to students that identifying negative thought patterns and thinking errors is only part of the process. Use an example to describe a process that involves the following:

1. Identifying (recognizing) a negative thought pattern

2. Making a decision regarding the validity of the thought (i.e., Is this based on a thinking error or on real evidence?)

3. Replacing or reframing the negative thought if it is based on a thinking error

### Sample Script

*We all have negative thoughts at some point. Sometimes the negative thoughts we have are normal reactions to bad situations. These negative thoughts help us make decisions about our safety and our choices. For example, you may have negative thoughts about failing a test. When you look for evidence about this type of "negative thought," you find that some thoughts could be true or reasonable. For example, it is reasonable to think you might fail a test if you did not study. On the other hand, if you studied really hard for the test, it is not reasonable to think that you will do poorly.*

 ## Activity A: Using Evidence

Use Supplement 7.2 as an overhead transparency to discuss using evidence to examine our thoughts. Help students understand the process of identifying a negative

thought using evidence to determine if the thought is reasonable. Review each situation, asking the following questions:

- What is the evidence?
- Is it realistic or reasonable?

### Sample Script

*We all remember what thinking errors look like and how they can lead to negative thoughts. So what can we do with our negative thoughts? Knowing that we are having a negative thought is just the beginning of the process. Next, we have to decide whether or not the negative thoughts are based on reasonable evidence. We can find evidence by asking ourselves questions about the negative thoughts. Here is how it would look if we wrote it down when we had a negative thought.*

Refer to Supplement 7.2 for examples.

## Activity B: Reframing

Use Supplement 7.3 as an overhead transparency to discuss how to identify thinking errors and how to use methods of reframing. Work through the examples, explaining the rationale behind the reframing process (i.e., reframing is simply an exercise that involves taking the same negative information and placing it into a more likely or realistic frame). Encourage discussion and input from the students regarding their experiences with negative thoughts.

### Sample Script

*In order to change the negative thoughts that come to mind in these types of situations, there are a couple of different activities you can do. One of the things to do is called reframing. Reframing means to turn the negative thoughts around by thinking about the situation differently. When you reframe something, you take the negative information and put it into a more realistic situation. Here are some examples of reframing*

Refer to Supplement 7.3.

Discuss with students how in some situations you may not have control or the ability to change the circumstances, while in other situations you may need to take responsibility for making changes in the situation.

## Activity C: Homework from Lesson 6

Use Supplement 7.4 as an overhead transparency, and ask students to take out their homework assignment from Lesson 6. Use students' examples to practice reframing. The students will see how reframing and identifying thinking errors can be useful in everyday situations. Use Supplement 7.4 to guide this process as a group activity.

### Sample Script

*We are going to use the homework you did last week when we talked about how to identify negative thoughts and thinking errors. We are going to use examples from that homework to practice reframing.*

Ask students to volunteer a negative thought based on their homework responses. Guide students through the Changing Thinking Errors process using the following steps:

1.  What was the negative thought?

2.  What is the evidence for or against the negative thought?

3.  Was there a thinking error? Yes or no?

4.  What was the thinking error?

5.  What is a more realistic way of thinking about it? (Reframing the thinking error)

If there is time, ask for volunteers from the class to role-play some of the homework examples. Have the students model situations in which negative thoughts could potentially have been reframed.

# Closure

Gather your students together, and review the lesson's main points. Close the lesson with a few thoughts to tie Lessons 6 and 7 together. These may be responses to questions the students have had or comments they made during the lesson. Be sure to encourage students to use these skills daily.

## Main Ideas

What are the steps of Changing Thinking Errors?

*   Identify negative thoughts.

*   Look for evidence for or against.

*   Decide if there was a thinking error. If so, which thinking error?

*   Use reframing to think about it realistically or more positively.

Use Supplement 7.5, Feelings Thermometer, as an overhead transparency for students to view.

### Sample Script

*Everyone has negative thoughts from time to time. Sometimes we have to think about our negative thoughts to decide if we should try to change them. We can use the thermometer to gauge our negative thoughts. If our negative thoughts are getting high, this could be a good time to use reframing. Sometimes negative thoughts cannot be reframed, and, in these cases, it is important to find something positive to focus on in order to take responsibility for our feelings and behaviors.*

# Homework Handout

Pass out the homework handout, Supplement 7.6. Explain how to fill in the columns. Encourage students to identify at least two events for the chart. Remind the students not to identify who they are referring to in the homework.

### Sample Script

*Just like the practice we did in class today (Supplement 7.4), for homework I would like you to think about more situations where negative thinking can be changed. You will be using the same form that we just used for our discussion.*

# Tips for Transfer Training

## Precorrect

Tell your students to use their knowledge of Clear Thinking to identify the opportunities to refute negative thinking throughout the day. Situations like report-card day or results to state and classroom assessments may be particularly good times to use this precorrection.

## Remind

If you notice students using one of the six types of negative thinking, ask them if they recognize what type of thinking they are using, and strategize effective ways to reframe the events and/or to examine the evidence that supports or refutes their thinking.

## Reinforce

Reward students observed identifying positive thinking opportunities. Catch and compliment students identifying and using evidence-based steps to reframe negative thinking.

 # Common Thinking Errors

**Binocular vision**
Looking at things in a way that makes them seem bigger or smaller than they really are

**Black-and-white thinking**
Looking at things in only extreme or opposite ways (for example, thinking of things as being good or bad, never or always, all or none)

**Dark glasses**
Thinking about only the negative parts of things

**Fortune-telling**
Making predictions about what will happen in the future without enough evidence

**Making it personal**
Blaming yourself for things that are not your fault

**Blame game**
Blaming others for things you should take responsibility for

*Strong Kids—Grades 3–5: A Social and Emotional Learning Curriculum*
by Kenneth W. Merrell, with assistance from Dianna Carrizales, Laura Feuerborn,
Barbara A. Gueldner, and Oanh K. Tran © 2007 University of Oregon. All rights reserved.

103

 **Evidence For or Against**

| Negative thought | What is the evidence? | | Is it realistic/ reasonable? |
|---|---|---|---|
| **A**<br><br>My friend never chooses me when it's time to choose sides for dodge ball. He hates me. | **For?**<br><br>Over the past week, whenever we've played dodge ball, Marcus has not chosen me for his team. | **Against?**<br><br>He plays with me at my house. We eat lunch together. He laughs at my jokes. He is really serious about dodge ball. I'm not. | If he hated me, he probably would not want to spend any time with me or even talk to me. |
| **B**<br><br>I am such an awful dancer. I will never make the dance team. I'm never good at anything. | **For?**<br><br>All of the other students are catching on to the dance steps. I keep falling. I have failed both tryouts. | **Against?**<br><br>I cannot predict the future. I can't be good at everything, and there are other things that I am better at. | The team leader has some very specific requirements for someone who makes the team, and, so far, I have not been able to do them. It is reasonable to expect that I might not make the dance team this time around. There are other activities I can join instead. |

*Strong Kids—Grades 3–5: A Social and Emotional Learning Curriculum*
by Kenneth W. Merrell, with assistance from Dianna Carrizales, Laura Feuerborn,
Barbara A. Gueldner, and Oanh K. Tran © 2007 University of Oregon. All rights reserved.

STRONG KID
LESSON

# Reframing Negative Thoughts

| What was my negative thought? | What thinking error did I make? | What is a more realistic way of thinking about it? (Reframe) |
|---|---|---|
| My friend never chooses me when it's time to choose sides for dodge ball. He hates me. | Black-and-white thinking | Marcus probably knows that I don't really like to play dodge ball, so he picks other people who like to play. |
| I am such an awful dancer. I will never make the dance team. | Fortune-telling | If I don't make the dance team, I still have other things I can do. |
| Everything at home is bad. | Dark glasses | Some things at home seem bad right now, but there are some good things, too. |
| It's awful that I fight so much with my dad. | Binocular vision | Most of the time I don't fight with my dad, just sometimes. |

*Strong Kids—Grades 3–5: A Social and Emotional Learning Curriculum*
by Kenneth W. Merrell, with assistance from Dianna Carrizales, Laura Feuerborn,
Barbara A. Gueldner, and Oanh K. Tran © 2007 University of Oregon. All rights reserved

 **Changing Thinking Errors**

| What was the negative thought? | What is the evidence (for or against)? | Was there a thinking error (yes or no)? | What was the thinking error? | What is a more realistic way of thinking about it? (Reframing) |
|---|---|---|---|---|
|  |  |  |  |  |

# Feelings Thermometer

High

Medium

Low

107

# Changing Thinking Errors

Name (optional): _____

**Directions:** Identify two situations where you can change negative thinking. Use the questions at the top of the chart to help you identify the negative thoughts and reframe these thoughts.

| What was the negative thought? | Was there a thinking error (yes or no)? | What was the thinking error? | What is a more realistic way of thinking about it? | What skill would I use? (Reframing) |
|---|---|---|---|---|
|  |  |  |  |  |

STRONG KID
LESSON

## LESSON 8

# The Power of Positive Thinking

**TEACHER NOTES**

_____
_____
_____
_____
_____
_____
_____
_____
_____
_____
_____
_____
_____
_____
_____
_____
_____
_____
_____

## Purpose

- To teach students how to change their negative thoughts and beliefs

## Objectives

- Students will accurately list the steps of the ABCDE Model of Learned Optimism.

- Students will be able to distinguish between examples and nonexamples of positive thinking.

- Students will apply the procedures of positive thinking to a classroom situation.

- Students will generalize or apply this lesson to real-life situations.

---

**MATERIALS NEEDED**

❑ Supplement 8.1 (overhead transparency)

❑ Supplement 8.2 (overhead transparency and homework handout)

❑ Supplement 8.3 (overhead transparency)

❑ Supplement 8.4 (overhead transparency)

**2–3 minutes** **Review**

To activate prior knowledge, review and discuss previous assignments and main ideas. Obtain 3–5 adequate ideas. Discuss with students their responses to last week's homework assignment.

### Sample Script

*During our last meeting, we discussed how to identify and change negative thoughts. Raise your hand if you can tell me an important idea we learned in our last class.*

### Ideas Discussed in Lesson 7

What are the steps of Changing Thinking?

- Identify negative thoughts.
- Look for evidence for or against.
- Decide if there was a thinking error. If so, which thinking error?
- Use reframing to think about it realistically or more positively.

**2 minutes** **Introduction**

Communicate the lesson's purpose and objectives clearly. Introduce the concept of positive thinking as a way of changing negative thoughts.

### Sample Script

*We are going to discuss positive thinking today. We will learn what this is and learn about ways that will help you identify and change the negative thoughts that you might have.*

**9–12 minutes** **Name and Define Skills**

### Activity A

Use Supplement 8.1 as an overhead transparency to discuss the relevant vocabulary. Provide examples to clarify important terms.

### Sample Script

*Here are some important terms that will help us understand the role of positive thinking to look at situations differently.*

- ***Self-control**—the ability to control your own behavior, especially in terms of your actions and impulses*
- ***Personal control**—believing that you have control over the important outcomes in your life*
- ***Optimism**—believing, expecting, or hoping that things will turn out well*
- ***Pessimism**—always expecting something bad to happen*

## Activity B

Convey the following main ideas to your students using your own words or use the sample script provided.

- Positive thinking is the act of viewing the world from a positive perspective, with expectations for pleasant and good outcomes and ready solutions.

- Positive thinking is a desirable trait for healthy minds.

- Negative thinking involves the generation of unhappy, angry, or unpleasant ideas in your thoughts.

- Negative thinking occurs sometimes but should not happen more often than positive or neutral thoughts.

### Sample Script

*Everyone has negative thoughts once in a while. Arguments with your parents, problems with your friends, or poor grades can all cause negative thoughts. It is important to remember that there should be a balance between positive and negative thoughts. One bad event should not ruin your whole day.*

Facilitate a class discussion about negative thinking and how to look at situations differently. The following questions and statements are provided to facilitate a discussion.

- Give reasons why you might have negative thoughts about yourself, your abilities, or your potential.

- Do these negative thoughts occur because you place too much blame on yourself?

- Do negative thoughts occur because you think you can't control what happens to you?

- Can you recognize situations where you can't control the outcome?

- Are there circumstances where you can control your feelings and behaviors?

- Do you think you could change your negative thoughts?

Emphasize that it is important to take credit for your successes and not blame yourself for bad things that happen, especially those that you can't control. This is a way to change your thinking and stop the negative thoughts.

# Introduce the ABCDE Model of Learned Optimism

Use Supplement 8.2, The ABCDE Model of Learned Optimism, as an overhead transparency. Introduce the model as a helpful tool to use to change negative thoughts into positive thinking. Discuss each component of the model.

### Sample Script

*This is the model that we will use to change negative thoughts into positive thinking. The **A** in the model stands for Adversity. Adversity means any problem or trouble in your life where you feel uncomfortable. Think about what problems you are likely to encounter at home and at school.*

*The **B** in the model stands for Belief. Beliefs are bad thoughts or hopeless thoughts that make you think things are your fault.*

*The **C** stands for Consequence. One consequence of bad thoughts is crummy feelings that you get in your head and that make you feel worse. Sometimes crummy feelings can sneak up on you, and you don't realize it until you feel bad.*

*The **D** stands for Deciding. This means deciding not to accept the negative or crummy thoughts that make you feel guilty. Look for and use hopeful and helpful beliefs that make you feel comfortable and competent. What can you say to yourself that will tell you to not think in those negative ways?*

*Finally, the **E** in the model stands for Energy. Energy means enjoying the idea that you can control what you think about yourself. How will you feel after you have replaced the negative thoughts with more positive ones?*

# Integrate and Illustrate the ABCDE Model

**15–18 minutes**

## Activity A: Cartoon Situation

Use Supplement 8.3, Cartoon Situation, as an overhead transparency to narrate and discuss the ABCDE model.

### Part 1: Discussion of Situation

Discuss the *A* (Adversity/Any Problem), *B* (Beliefs/Bad Thoughts), and *C* (Consequence/Crummy Feelings) parts of the ABCDE model. Use the following prompt to start the discussion.

### Sample Script

- *What is the A part of the ABCDE model? In other words, what is your Adversity or problem in this situation?*

  Answers include "I suggested playing Checkers; everyone laughed and said, 'Naaaaww!'"

- *What is the B part of the ABCDE model? In other words, what Beliefs or Bad thoughts might you have in this situation?*

  Answers include "My friends don't like me" and "My friends don't want to play with me."

- *What is the C part of the ABCDE model? In other words, what is the Consequence or the Crummy feeling that you might experience after having those beliefs or bad thoughts?*

  Answers include "I feel awful" and "I feel stupid."

## Part 2: Explore Possible Negative Responses to the Situation

Discuss additional thoughts and feelings the students might have in that situation. Emphasize that thoughts and feelings aren't always limited to just a few and can continue to occur. These thoughts and feelings can become troubling to some people when they keep happening and do not stop.

### Sample Response

*You suddenly wish you hadn't suggested Checkers. While your friends have moved on and are still discussing what game to play, you are still thinking about how stupid everyone must think you are. You think that things like this always happen to you and that if you were smarter or more popular, you could have come up with a better idea. These thoughts keep replaying in your head over and over again.*

## Part 3: Explore Alternative Ways to Think about the Situation

Generate alternative ways to look at the situation. Below are some possibilities. Use the following prompt to start the discussion. Emphasize the idea that you can control the thoughts that you have about yourself.

### Sample Script

*How could you use the D part of the ABCDE model to decide about your negative thoughts and not get so upset about them? In other words, how could you decide to think about the situation differently?*

Answers include the following:

1. You could have decided that there was nothing wrong with your suggestion of Checkers and that:

   - Your friends should have responded more pleasantly even if they did not agree.

   - Your friends were not being mean. They were just eager to get a game they all agreed on.

   - You are making a big deal out of nothing because everyone else has stopped talking about it.

2. You could have decided that, in hindsight, Checkers was not the best suggestion because [you always play Checkers, there's only one checkerboard, no one else knows how to play Checkers, you only have 5 minutes].

3. You could laugh or shrug it off because everyone makes mistakes once in a while.

### Sample Script

*How do you think the E part of the ABCDE model would apply to you after deciding to think about the situation differently? In other words, would you feel Energized and Enjoy the idea that you can control what you think about yourself?*

## Activity B: Create a Situation

Encourage students to think of a situation that might happen that could elicit negative thoughts. Create and modify suggestions, making them relevant to your students or relating them to topics that are current in your classroom. Piece together the situation by asking questions like the following:

1. Where might you be?

2. Who might you be with?

3. What might be the situation/what's going on?

4. What might be your response/what do you do?

5. How do the others respond to you?

 Walk through the situation that you created using the ABCDE model to demonstrate the use of positive thinking. Use Supplement 8.2 to guide this discussion. Have students identify each component in the model (Adversity, Belief, Consequence, Deciding, Energy).

**5 minutes**

## Activity C: Learned Optimism Training (Optional)

If there is time, process another ABCDE situation to promote fluency.

### *Nonexample of Using the ABCDE Model (Negative Thinking)*

#### *Sample Script*

- **<u>A</u>dversity** *(Any problem)—Michelle answers a question wrong during a math activity.*

- **<u>B</u>elief** *(Bad thoughts)—Michelle believes the teacher is angry and the whole class thinks she is stupid.*

- **<u>C</u>onsequence** *(Crummy feelings)—Michelle feels depressed and thinks, "I wish I could run out of this classroom and never have to come back here again."*

  *As a result of not using Part D and Part E of the ABCDE model, Michelle stops raising her hand in class and feels nervous every day in math class, even when she knows the right answer.*

### *Example of Using the ABCDE Model (Positive Thinking)*

#### *Sample Script*

- **<u>A</u>dversity** *(Any problem)—Michelle answers a question wrong during a math activity.*

- **<u>B</u>elief** *(Bad thoughts)—Michelle believes the teacher is angry and the whole class thinks she is stupid.*

- **<u>C</u>onsequence** *(Crummy feelings)—Michelle feels depressed and thinks, "I wish I could run out of this classroom and never have to come back here again."*

- **_D_eciding** *(Decide not to accept crummy feelings and bad thoughts)—Michelle thinks, "Okay, I answered the question wrong, but that doesn't mean the teacher is mad. We are just learning these equations, and she can't expect that all of the students will always answer the questions right. The other kids in the class probably don't think I'm stupid because they get questions wrong, too, sometimes."*

- **_E_nergy** *(Enjoy)—Michelle thinks, "I'm still a little embarrassed about getting the question wrong, but I don't think the teacher is mad and the kids think I am stupid anymore. I no longer wish that I could run out of the classroom."*

# Closure

Use Supplement 8.4 as an overhead transparency to conduct an informal assessment of the students' understanding of the topic. Call on students to respond to the questions.

### Sample Script

*We are going to review some of the main ideas discussed in today's lesson. Raise your hand if you know some of these ideas.*

- *What is optimism about?*

  Optimism is about feeling good or positive about events and expecting good outcomes.

- *What is pessimism about?*

  Pessimism is about feeling bad or negative about events and expecting bad things to happen.

- *What is thinking positively?*

  Thinking positively is learning how to choose a different way of thinking about things so that you don't end up feeling miserable and sad whenever something doesn't work out for you.

- *What is one way to think positively?*

  One way to start thinking positively is by not taking all of the responsibility for bad outcomes and by not refusing all of the praise for good outcomes. Positive thinking has a lot to do with deciding where we have control in our lives and how we can change our thoughts.

- *How can we feel better about ourselves?*

  We can feel better about ourselves by taking responsibility when good things happen and attributing good things to something good about ourselves.

- *What are some ways you can make positive thinking work?*

  Positive thinking can work when you realize that you are not entirely to blame for everything that goes wrong. Take a few minutes to think about what has gone wrong, instead of immediately blaming yourself. You will see that some parts of the situation were probably out of your control. (When things go wrong, it doesn't mean you are a bad person.)

*Positive thinking can also work when you realize that when things **do** go right, you can **and should** take some of the credit, instead of supposing that it was a lucky break.*

*It can work when you realize that, even when you have to take responsibility or blame for some negative event, you always learn something new and positive for the future.*

If there is time, engage the students in a discussion over these two additional questions:

- Is it ever okay to have negative thoughts?

- What do you think happens when you have too many bad thoughts?

# Homework Handout

Use Supplement 8.2 as a homework handout, and distribute a copy to each student. Ask students to keep a journal of situations where they felt badly. Ask them to write about those situations, their reactions to those situations, and what they learned from those situations. They can apply the ABCDE model to help change the negative thinking.

*Note*: Consider in advance what will work best for your situation on the feelings journal activity. Consider whether students should do the journal activity only at home to protect their privacy or whether it would be okay to have them bring it to school. Also, consider what they should use for their journal, such as a spiral notebook or something made specifically in class for that purpose.

### Sample Script

*Your homework assignment for this week is to keep a journal for a week. Write about situations that happened during the week where you felt bad. Use the ABCDE model to think through the situations and how you felt. Write about how you reacted to each situation and why, who you blamed and why, and what you learned from the situations or any of your mistakes. I will not read the journals because they are private; however, for our next meeting, you can use your journal entries to write about one situation where something didn't go your way or you learned from your mistake. Use the ABCDE model to help you think through the situation.*

# Tips for Transfer Training

## Precorrect

Prior to situations involving the potential for stress and fear of failure, such as examinations, evaluations, and some competitions, tell your students to think of the positive thoughts that make them feel better and to use those thoughts when they feel as if crummy feelings might be taking over.

## Remind

If you notice students succumbing to negative thoughts, remind them that they have control of the thoughts in their head and that they can choose to change the thoughts or replace them with positive thoughts. Assure them that they can attribute a positive thought even to negative situations.

## Reinforce

For students who you know are braving situations that are difficult for them, ask them what strategies they used to get through these situations, and reinforce them for their efforts. For example, "Luke, you made it through the test. I know you were really nervous. How did you get through it?" After the student's response, reinforce his or her behavior with a compliment such as "Great job."

## Definitions

### Self-control

The ability to control your own behavior, especially in terms of your actions and impulses

### Personal control

Believing that you have control over the important outcomes in your life

### Optimism

Believing, expecting, or hoping that things will turn out well

### Pessimism

Always expecting something bad to happen

# The ABCDE Model of Learned Optimism

### Changing Negative Thoughts Using an ABCDE Model

## Adversity

Any problem or situation where you feel uncomfortable

## Belief

Bad thoughts or negative thoughts that make you think things are your fault

## Consequence

Crummy feelings that you get in your head that make you feel worse. Sometimes crummy feelings can sneak up on you, and you don't realize it until you feel bad.

## Deciding

Deciding not to accept the negative or crummy thoughts that make you feel guilty. Look for and use hopeful and helpful beliefs that make you feel comfortable and competent. What can you say to yourself that will tell you to not think in those negative ways?

## Energy

Enjoying the idea that you can control what you think about yourself. How will you feel after you have replaced the negative thoughts with more positive ones?

119

 **Cartoon Situation**

### Any problem

You are in the classroom during free time with your friends. You are all deciding what game you should play next. Everyone is contributing ideas when . . .

Suddenly, you suggest Checkers!!

But everyone laughs and says, "Naaaw!!" and you end up feeling awful. It feels like they don't like you and they just don't want to play with you. You feel stupid for suggesting Checkers.

### Bad thoughts

### Crummy feelings

Fortunately, you remember to dispute the negative thoughts with some hopeful and helpful thoughts.

### Decide not to accept the crummy feelings and bad thoughts!

Finally, you decide to enjoy the energized feeling that you get from positive thinking.

### Enjoy!

*Strong Kids—Grades 3–5: A Social and Emotional Learning Curriculum*
by Kenneth W. Merrell, with assistance from Dianna Carrizales, Laura Feuerborn,
Barbara A. Gueldner, and Oanh K. Tran © 2007 University of Oregon. All rights reserved.

 **Let's Talk About What We Know**

1. Is optimism positive or negative?

2. What is optimism about?

3. What is pessimism about?

4. What is thinking positive?

5. What is one way to start thinking positive?

6. How can we feel better about ourselves?

7. What are some ways I can make positive thinking work?

8. Is it ever okay to have negative thoughts?

9. What happens if I have too many bad thoughts?

**LESSON 9**

# Solving People Problems

**TEACHER NOTES**

## ★ Purpose

- To teach students to solve conflicts with other people

## ★ Objectives

- Students will accurately list steps of a social Problem-Solving Model.

- Students will be able to distinguish between positive and negative examples of social problem solving.

- Students will apply the procedures of social problem solving to a classroom situation.

- Students will generalize or apply this lesson to real-life situations.

---

**MATERIALS NEEDED**

- ❏ Supplement 9.1 (overhead transparency and in-class handout)
- ❏ Supplement 9.2 (overhead transparency and in-class handout)
- ❏ Supplement 9.3 (overhead transparency)
- ❏ Supplement 9.4 (homework handout)
- ❏ Optional Supplement: Role-Play Activities (overhead transparency)

**2–5 minutes**

# Review

To activate prior knowledge, review and discuss previous topics and main ideas. Obtain 3–5 adequate ideas. If appropriate, ask students for examples from their journal entries from last week's homework assignment.

### Sample Script

*During our last meeting, we discussed ways of changing our negative thoughts into more realistic or positive thoughts. Raise your hand if you can tell me an important idea or an example of positive thinking.*

## Ideas Discussed in Lesson 8

- What are the definitions of *self-control*, *personal control*, *optimism*, and *pessimism?*
- Explain the concepts of positive thinking and negative thinking.
- Experiencing negative thoughts is normal.
- How can the ABCDE model change negative thoughts into positive thinking?

**2–5 minutes**

# Introduction

Communicate the lesson's purpose and objectives clearly. Introduce the concept of conflict resolution, or social problem solving.

### Sample Script

*Today, we will learn a skill called conflict resolution or, as it is sometimes called, problem solving. We will learn how to use conflict resolution. We will learn what it looks like, and then we will all practice conflict resolution step by step.*

**5 minutes**

# Name and Define Skills

Use Supplement 9.1 as an overhead transparency and in-class handout to define the relevant terms.

### Sample Script

*Here are some important terms that will help us understand problem solving.*

- ***Conflict/problem***—*a disagreement or something that doesn't match or work well together*
- ***Resolution***—*the part where we (try to) resolve the conflict or find a solution*
- ***Resolve***—*to fix, mend, or solve*
- ***Problem solving/conflict resolution***—*a way of discussing a topic in a helpful/constructive manner and finding some way to reach an agreement*

# Understanding Conflict

Convey the following main ideas to your students using your own words or the sample scripts.

## Main Idea 1: Conflict

- Not all conflicts are bad. They can be neutral or good.
- They are inherent with human behavior, and you should learn from conflicts.
- Conflict does not have to end with a "winner" and a "loser." The aim is to end the conflict with all people satisfied with the outcome.

### Sample Script

*Problems are sometimes called conflicts or disagreements. Conflicts or disagreements are not necessarily bad. In fact, they can be opportunities to learn about a person or situation. All problems or disagreements do not have to end up with one person winning and one person losing. Conflicts can be solved by understanding both people's views and perspectives, agreeing to disagree, or compromising. Conflict resolution is a way to solve our problems or disagreements one step at a time. For example, you and a classmate are working on a poster and you disagree on the pictures to put on it. Since you know that you both should consider the other person's perspectives, you compromise and put pictures that both people like.*

## Main Idea 2: Alternatives to Conflict

Use Supplement 9.2 as an overhead transparency and in-class handout to discuss alternatives to conflict.

### Sample Script

*There are many ways to resolve conflicts:*

- ***Compromise**—One or both parties agree to some level of sacrifice in order to prevent a continued conflict.*
- ***Agreement**—One party decides that the other party's point of view is relevant and they can agree to share the same point of view.*
- ***Agree to disagree**—Both parties feel that there is no way to agree on the topic and will decide that it is a topic that they have differing perspectives on. Having differing perspectives is okay!*
- ***Friendly rivalry/Leave it to chance**—Sometimes, if the conflict is over something tangible, the two parties can agree to have a competition over the object (e.g., game of Chess winner gets the object, flipping a coin).*
- ***Seeking guidance from a responsible party or elder**—Sometimes adults have to be called in to make the decision.*
- ***Making a deal**—Sometimes an agreement can be reached by making a deal (e.g., "If I do this, will you do that?")*

# Problem-Solving
# Model for Conflict Resolution

Describe conflict resolution as a way to solve problems or disagreements one step at a time.

## Activity A

Use Supplement 9.3 as an overhead transparency to discuss the four-step Problem-Solving Model for conflict resolution.

### Sample Script

*There are four steps in the Problem-Solving Model.*

1. ***Identify the problem**—What are you arguing about?*

    - *Have the other person state his or her wants and feelings.*

    - *Use active and empathetic listening skills.*

    - *Read the other person's body language.*

    - *Describe, in a nonthreatening way, what you want using "I" statements.*

    - *Describe how you feel.*

    - *Summarize both people's wants and feelings.*

2. ***Brainstorm solutions**—List some of the ways you can solve this problem. Each person should generate at least two solutions.*

3. ***Choose a solution**—Which way seems the most reasonable to everyone?*

    - *Does it work for all involved?*

    - *Is it a win-win situation?*

    - *Is someone willing to compromise?*

    - *If no agreement can be reached, go back to the previous step, Brainstorming Solutions.*

    - *It is important to be open minded and respectful instead of being mean or sarcastic during the Brainstorming Solutions step. Consider all of the solutions.*

4. ***Make an agreement**—All people must accept the terms of the solution. Jointly accept a solution, and formalize it with a handshake or contract.*

## Activity B

Brainstorm ways to use problem solving during a conflict.

*Sample Script*

*Sometimes conflicts can seem really confusing and impossible to solve. At times like that, it is hard to think about the problem without feeling hurt. Sometimes it's even hard to figure out what the conflict is exactly. Let's see how we can brainstorm some ways to use problem solving during a conflict situation.*

Emphasize the following examples of statements that can be used during conflict resolution:

- "I need a minute to think about this."

- "Wait, let's figure out what we're arguing about."

- "Listen, I don't want to argue with you. Let's think about this for a while."

- "Okay, you want this, and I want this. Let's see if we can think of a way so that we can both have it."

Discuss the idea that conflicts are challenging and using problem-solving or conflict-resolution strategies requires patience and creativity!

*Sample Script*

*Sometimes, even trying your very best to find a solution doesn't work. Or sometimes, if everyone doesn't know about the four steps to problem solving, it can turn into a bigger argument. In those situations, you may have to smile, be patient, and politely say, "I hear what you are saying, but let's talk about this another time and try again to solve the problem."*

# Integrate Key Concepts

This section can be taught separately or woven in throughout your lesson via the example situations, modeling situations, or the student role-play situations (see Optional Supplement: Role-Play Activities).

Discuss a current event that can be associated or even improved with problem solving (e.g., recent news headline). Ask students to use the Problem-Solving Model to discuss the situation. Discuss the importance of respecting differences in perspectives and opinions. Discuss how negative thinking or not empathizing with other's feelings or perspectives can be a roadblock to effective problem solving. As a consequence, people are less able to listen, use empathy skills, and compromise.

# Modeling

Use your own example or one of the examples provided, and model a situation to the class. You can use a student volunteer or act out both roles involved in the situation. Optional Supplement: Role-Play Activities (overhead transparency) at the end of this lesson contains two additional role-play situations.

### Situation 1

*Your classmate wants to use the only class computer at the same time you do. Identify the problem, discuss each person's wants and needs, and come to an agreement to share the computer.*

### Situation 2

*Your classmate has broken your trust by telling a secret of yours. Discuss the problem, discuss each person's wants and needs, and come to an agreement that one apologizes and agrees to never do that again—or risk losing a friendship. The other person forgives the friend.*

## Examples and Nonexamples of Problem Solving

Based on your knowledge of your students, use current and realistic conflicts to practice problem solving. Have students give examples and nonexamples of problem-solving strategies. Integrate a discussion about school rules, house rules, and dangerous problem-solving situations. The problem-solving skills students have just learned may be inappropriate in some situations. For example, in a life-threatening situation, a problem-solving discussion with a potentially dangerous individual may not be appropriate.

## Sample Problem

Consider the following problem: Two students want the same ball during physical education. Choose some of the following potential solutions, and prompt students with the question: Is this an example of problem solving or not an example of problem solving? For the items that are nonexamples of problem solving, ask students how they would use problem-solving skills to resolve the conflict.

### Sample Script

*Let's consider the conflict of two students who want to use the same ball during physical education. Let's discuss some ways this conflict could be resolved and decide whether these are examples of problem solving.*

### Situation 1 (Example)

*The students identify the problem, clarify their wants, brainstorm solutions, agree to equally split the time each uses the ball, and shake hands.*

### Situation 2 (Nonexample)

*The students argue, interrupt each other, and one student tells the teacher.*

### Situation 3 (Nonexample)

*The students identify the problem, clarify wants, and brainstorm solutions, but then they can't agree to a solution.*

*Situation 4 (Nonexample)*

*The students identify the problem but stay fixed on the second step of problem solving. They're focused on what they want and disregard what the other person wants.*

*Situation 5 (Example)*

*The students identify the problem, clarify wants, brainstorm solutions, agree to use the ball on different days, and give one another their "word."*

# Closure

Gather your students together, and review the lesson's main points.

- Define *conflict/problem*, *resolution*, *resolve*, and *problem-solving/conflict resolution*.

- What are some alternatives to conflict?

- Describe the four-step Problem-Solving Model.

- What statements can you use during conflict resolution?

- Conflict resolution/problem solving requires patience and creativity.

    *Sample Script*

    *Today, we learned a skill called problem solving, or conflict resolution. We learned the steps of the Problem-Solving Model and how to use those steps in everyday situations. When you have a problem, decide if you can resolve it together using the problem-solving strategies we talked about today. Define the conflict together, try to see the problem as the other person would, and suggest several things you could do to solve the problem. Everyone should agree to the solution. Look for opportunities to practice conflict resolution during problems at home, at school, and with your friends.*

# Homework Handout

Pass out the homework handout, Supplement 9.4, Resolving Conflicts. Tell students that they are asked to use the Problem-Solving Model to work through a problem in the past and to provide a new ending to the problem.

# Tips for Transfer Training

## Precorrect

Prior to situations requiring group work or activities, remind students to use their people problem-solving skills to resolve any disagreements of ideas that may come up. Remind them to identify the problem, brainstorm solutions, and choose a solution to agree on.

## Remind

If you happen upon a situation where students are involved in a conflict, remind students to brainstorm solutions and to listen to each other. Tell them you will be back in 5 minutes to see how the situation was resolved.

## Reinforce

For students using problem-solving skills to brainstorm solutions in social situations, reinforce the behavior by specifying what you observed and complimenting the process. For example, "Great job, Natalie. I really like the way you stated all of the options and helped the group to brainstorm to this great solution."

# Definitions

## Conflict/problem

A disagreement that occurs between two or more people, or two or more groups of people. It can be a difference of opinion, a difference in goals, a difference in desires, or a difference in ability. Sometimes, the difference is a completely opposing point of view.

## Resolution

Finding a solution; resolving the problem

## Resolve

To fix, mend, or solve

## Problem solving/conflict resolution

A way of discussing a topic in a helpful/constructive manner, finding some way of reaching an agreement in the best way for most of the people

131

 **Alternatives to Conflict**

## Compromise

One or both parties agree to some level of sacrifice to prevent a continued conflict.

## Agreement

One party decides that the other party's point of view is relevant and they can agree to share the same point of view.

## Agree to disagree

Both parties feel that there is no way to agree on the topic and will decide that it is a topic that they have differing perspectives on. Having differing perspectives is okay!

## Friendly rivalry/Leave it to chance

The two parties agree to compete over the object (e.g., game of Chess winner gets the object, flipping a coin).

## Seeking guidance from a responsible party or elder

Adults are called in to make the decision.

## Making a deal

Sometimes an agreement can be reached by making a deal (e.g., "Okay, what if I give you this? Can we switch turns now?").

*Strong Kids—Grades 3–5: A Social and Emotional Learning Curriculum*
by Kenneth W. Merrell, with assistance from Dianna Carrizales, Laura Feuerborn,
Barbara A. Gueldner, and Oanh K. Tran © 2007 University of Oregon. All rights reserved.

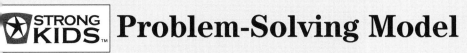

# Problem-Solving Model

## Step 1—Identify the problem

Have the other person state his or her wants and feelings.

Use empathy and active listening skills.

Read the other person's body language.

Describe your wants and feelings using "I" statements.

Describe how you feel.

Summarize both people's wants and feelings.

## Step 2—Brainstorm solutions

Each person should generate at least two solutions.

## Step 3—Choose a solution

Does it work for all involved?

Is it a win–win situation?

Is someone willing to compromise?

If no agreement can be reached, go back to the previous step.

## Step 4—Make an agreement

All people must accept the terms of the solution and formalize the solution with a handshake or a written contract.

*Strong Kids—Grades 3–5: A Social and Emotional Learning Curriculum*
by Kenneth W. Merrell, with assistance from Dianna Carrizales, Laura Feuerborn,
Barbara A. Gueldner, and Oanh K. Tran © 2007 University of Oregon. All rights reserved.

133

Your sister got into your CD collection. Last week, you asked her not to do this, but she went into your room, got into the collection, and left a big mess. Now, one of your CDs is missing. What should you do?

**Steps to the Problem-Solving Model**

1. *Identify the problem*—What are we arguing about?

2. *Brainstorm solutions*—Let's list some of the ways we can solve this problem.

3. *Choose a solution*—Which way seems the most reasonable to everyone?

4. *Make an agreement*—All people must accept the terms of the solution.

You are watching your favorite television show. Your brother comes in and changes the channel to watch something that he really likes, and it is showing only this one time. There is only one television in the house. What should you do?

**Steps to the Problem-Solving Model**

1. *Identify the problem*—What are we arguing about?

2. *Brainstorm solutions*—Let's list some of the ways we can solve this problem.

3. *Choose a solution*—Which way seems the most reasonable to everyone?

4. *Make an agreement*—All people must accept the terms of the solution.

*Strong Kids—Grades 3–5: A Social and Emotional Learning Curriculum*
by Kenneth W. Merrell, with assistance from Dianna Carrizales, Laura Feuerborn,
Barbara A. Gueldner, and Oanh K. Tran © 2007 University of Oregon. All rights reserved.

134

STRONG KI

LESSON

# Resolving Conflicts

Name (optional): _____

**Directions:** Think of a problem or conflict that you had with a person in the past. How did you handle it? How could you have handled it better? Use the problem-solving steps you learned today and provide a *new ending* to this problem or conflict. Refer to Supplement 9.2 for ideas on "alternatives to conflict."

Step 1—Identify the problem.

_____

_____

_____

Step 2—Brainstorm solutions.

_____

_____

_____

Step 3—Choose a solution.

_____

_____

_____

Step 4—Make an agreement (new ending).

_____

_____

_____

*Strong Kids—Grades 3–5: A Social and Emotional Learning Curriculum*
by Kenneth W. Merrell, with assistance from Dianna Carrizales, Laura Feuerborn,
Barbara A. Gueldner, and Oanh K. Tran © 2007 University of Oregon. All rights reserved.                135

# Letting Go of Stress

**TEACHER NOTES**

## ⭐ Purpose

- To teach students methods to identify and reduce stress

## ⭐ Objectives

- Students will learn to identify signs of stress in themselves and others.
- Students will learn about situations that might cause stress.
- Students will learn the difference between positive and negative ways of coping with stress.
- Students will identify and choose specific methods that can reduce stress.
- Students will generalize or apply this lesson to real-life situations.

| MATERIALS NEEDED |
|---|

- ❑ Supplement 10.1 (overhead transparency and in-class handout)
- ❑ Supplement 10.2 (in-class handout)
- ❑ Supplement 10.3 (homework handout)

**2–3 minutes**

# Review

To activate prior knowledge, review and discuss previous topics and main ideas. Obtain 3–5 adequate ideas. Discuss with students their responses to last week's homework assignment.

### Sample Script

*During our last meeting, we discussed ways to solve problems. Raise your hand if you can tell me an important idea we learned in our last class.*

## Ideas Discussed in Lesson 9

- Define *conflict/problem, resolution, resolve,* and *problem-solving/conflict resolution.*
- What are some alternatives to conflict?
- Describe the four-step Problem-Solving Model.
- What statements can you use during conflict resolution?
- Conflict resolution/problem solving requires patience and creativity.

**2 minutes**

# Introduction

Communicate the lesson's purpose and objectives clearly. Introduce the concept of stress as being a normal part of being human. There are healthy ways of dealing with stress.

### Sample Script

*Today, we will talk about stress. Stress is part of being human, and people deal with it in different ways. It is important to find healthy ways of dealing with it instead of ways that will cause more problems in the future. Many of the things we worry about can be handled by using healthy strategies to deal with stress. We'll talk about different situations that make us feel stressed out and find ways of dealing with stress that will work.*

**5 minutes**

# Name and Define Skills

## Activity A

Use Supplement 10.1 as an overhead transparency and in-class handout to discuss and define the following important concepts:

- *Stress*—A feeling of being overwhelmed that can happen before, during, or after a difficult situation. You can also feel stressed or overwhelmed when you have too much to do or when you are trying to concentrate on something important and you feel distracted and nervous inside.

- *Common signs of stress*—Body or hands shake, fists clench, teeth and jaws clench up, muscles tighten, feeling like you can't do it, feeling tired, irritability, scared/worried/nervous

- *Relax*—A feeling of letting go of stress. You can do this by physically loosening tense muscles or finding a way to deal with or ignore the things that are bothering or overwhelming you.

## Activity B

Convey the following main ideas to your students using your own words.

- Not all stress is bad—it can help you recognize that it is time to make a decision.

- Different situations may or may not be stressful for different people.

- Experiencing stress and not taking action to cope with it can eventually lead to negative physical and psychological outcomes.

# Identifying Feelings of Stress

Ask students to generate examples of stressful situations in their lives. Situations are also provided to use as examples. Encourage students to describe the situation, how they felt, and how they could tell they were feeling stress. Remind students not to offer solutions.

### Sample Script

*There are some times when people never feel stress and other times when most people feel stress. Some people might find one situation stressful, and others may not. Some might feel more stress because they are having a bad day. Describe times in your life when you felt stressed. What did it feel like? How could you tell that you were feeling stress?*

## Situations

If necessary, modify the situations to make them more relevant to your students. Read the situations, and ask students to model their reactions or probe students to explain how they would feel. Students should be able to relate to some of the signs of stress and see that other students may feel differently in stressful situations. Remind students to focus on feelings and not offer solutions.

### Situation 1 (School Example)

*Fred forgot that he had a vocabulary test today and didn't study for it. The teacher passes out the test, and Fred sits and stares at his test. What is he feeling?*

### Situation 2 (Social Example)

*During a school assembly, Mariko is sitting next to her best friend. ʹ then moves and sits next to a group of other friends and gives ʹ look. What is she feeling?*

*Situation 3 (Community Example)*

*Sherrie was out shopping with her mom and stopped by the CD section. When she finished looking at the CDs, she turned to leave, and she didn't see her mom anywhere in the store. What is she feeling?*

## 5 minutes Dealing with Stress

Generate additional situations or use those provided in the previous section to brainstorm both negative and positive ways to deal with stress. Ask the students how they would know whether a solution is positive or negative.

### *Sample Script*

*Now that we know what stress is and when we might feel it, we can focus on ways to deal with stress. There are negative and positive ways to react to stress. Let's talk about negative and positive ways that people could handle the situations we just discussed.*

### *Situation 1 (School Example)*

*Fred forgot to study for his vocabulary test. What are some negative ways he could deal with his stress? What are some positive ways?*

### *Situation 2 (Social Example)*

*Mariko's best friend leaves her and goes to sit with a group of other friends and gives here a bad look during a school assembly. What are some negative ways she could deal with her stress? What are some positive ways?*

### *Situation 3 (Community Example)*

*Sherrie could not find her mom in the store. What are some negative ways she could deal with her stress? What are some positive ways?*

## 8 minutes Discussion

### Activity A

Help students generate specific ways they can relax when they are stressed or are about to encounter a stressful situation. Encourage them to share what they have used in the past or might try. In your discussion, solicit the following coping skills, but list all of the ideas suggested by the students, even those you may consider negative or counterproductive (e.g., alcohol, other drugs). If students do not mention them, consider listing them on the board as things some people do to reduce stress. The next step will be to evaluate them.

### *Sample Script*

*Let's talk about some ways to relax, or let go of stress. What are some things you could try when you're feeling stress or know you're about to get into a stressful situation? Think of things that you've done when you feel stressed. I'll write them up on the board, and we'll discuss them when we have enough good ideas.*

Examples of ways of dealing with stress:

- Talking about the problem with friends
- Physical activity (exercise, skateboarding, dancing)
- Focus in on something that you can change
- Facing the source of your fears instead of worrying about it
- Refer to Clear Thinking exercises covered in Lesson 6 (consider thinking errors, how to change negative thoughts)
- Using alcohol or other drugs (if appropriate to mention to your students)
- Getting angry at your family or friends

## Activity B

Focus on each strategy we listed, and evaluate each one for its effectiveness in reducing stress. For each strategy, ask students to consider whether the strategy will cause them more stress in the future.

### Sample Script

*We know that some ways of coping with stress are effective and some are not. Many ways that are not effective may work in the moment but have a tendency to make things worse in the long run. For each of the strategies we listed, ask yourself the question, "Will this cause me more stress in the long run?"*

When dealing with alcohol and other drugs, be prepared to name ways these methods could cause more trouble in the future (e.g., addiction, poor judgment with decision making, problems in relationships, physical illness, increases in risky behavior, accidents). Provide the names and numbers of local agencies if students need help with these issues for themselves or their friends and family.

# Activity

The following activity is a relaxation exercise, which may or may not be appropriate for all students. Take into account the specific needs of the group when deciding whether or not to include this activity in the lesson. Consider making it optional so that only students who are interested and will take it seriously may participate.

Provide students with the in-class handout Supplement 10.2, which describes a relaxation exercise that includes brief muscle relaxation while concentrating on breathing (adapted from Merrell, K.W. [2001] *Helping students overcome depression and anxiety: A practical guide.* New York: Guilford Press). Have students do this exercise in a quiet, comfortable place. Dim the lights if appropriate.

### Sample Script

*We are going to try a specific relaxation exercise. Try it, and see if it is helpful for you to relax.*

1. *Find a place that is not too noisy, a place where you feel comfortable closing your eyes.*

2. *When you find a quiet spot, sit or lie down in a comfortable position.*

3.  *Close your eyes.*

4.  *Listen to your breathing. Draw in deep, full breaths. Let them out slowly, and feel yourself relax as you breathe out.*

5.  *Breathe in, and tighten your leg muscles. Breathe out and relax. Breathe in and tighten your arm muscles. Breathe out and relax. Breathe in and tighten your face muscles. Breathe out and relax. Notice how calm they feel as you let them relax.*

6.  *Continue breathing in and out. Take slow, deep breaths.*

7.  *Think about being in a favorite place and being very relaxed and calm. If something is bothering you even when you are trying to relax, imagine putting your worries in a box on a high shelf.*

8.  *Stay quiet for a few minutes or as long as you need.*

## Closure

Gather your students together, and review the lesson's main points.

*   Stress is a normal part of being human.
*   Describe the common signs of stress.
*   Identify how you feel when stressed.
*   Identify positive and negative ways of reacting to stress.
*   Evaluate whether a strategy will cause more stress in the future.
*   Describe one relaxation exercise.

### Sample Script

*Today, we learned about stress and relaxation. Everyone feels stress differently. If you're feeling stress, think about some of the ways to relax using strategies that we talked about. Remember that there are positive and negative ways to deal with stress, which can help you or make things worse in the long run. We learned how to recognize stress and deal with it in positive ways. Try to use some of these ways to relax in your lives this week.*

## Homework Handout

Pass out the homework handout, Supplement 10.3, Letting Go of Stress. Students are asked to write about situations where they felt stressed, choose strategies that work for them, plan for an anticipated stressor, and choose a relaxation technique.

# Tips for Transfer Training

## Precorrect

Wherever appropriate, remind students to identify situations where their bodies may respond to stress before they are aware of it. Prior to stressful situations, such as spelling bees, poster sessions, and large-scale assessments, remind students to be on the lookout for physical signs of stress such as tense muscles, shaking hands, and rapid breathing and to find a way to address it that is consistent with the situation, such as slow breathing, muscle relaxation, or talking it out.

## Remind

If you notice a student responding physically to stress, or if you become aware of a student prone to stressful responses, remind the student to relax, use self-talk, and specify a possible appropriate method such as muscle relaxation, positive thinking, or slow breathing.

## Reinforce

When you observe a student using relaxation techniques to respond to stress, specify the technique and compliment the student for using it. For example, "Good job, Laura. I know you were really nervous, and I saw you using the slow breathing to relax. That's a great strategy."

# Definitions

## Stress

A feeling of being overwhelmed that can happen before, during, or after a difficult situation. You can also feel stressed or overwhelmed when you have too much to do or when you are trying to concentrate on something important and you feel distracted and nervous inside.

## Common signs of stress

- Body or hands shake
- Fists clench
- Teeth clench up
- Muscles tighten
- Feeling like you can't do it
- Feeling tired
- Irritability
- Scared/worried/nervous

## Relax

A feeling of letting go of stress. You can do this by physically loosening tense muscles or finding a way to deal with or ignore the things that are bothering or overwhelming you.

*Strong Kids—Grades 3–5: A Social and Emotional Learning Curriculum*
by Kenneth W. Merrell, with assistance from Dianna Carrizales, Laura Feuerborn,
Barbara A. Gueldner, and Oanh K. Tran © 2007 University of Oregon. All rights reserved.

STRONG KI
LESSON

# ★ STRONG KIDS™ Let Go of Stress!

When you find yourself feeling stressed, go through the following steps. At the end, you may find your muscles relaxed and your mind clear.

1.  Find a place that is not too noisy, a place where you feel comfortable closing your eyes.

2.  When you find a quiet spot, sit or lie down in a comfortable position.

3.  Close your eyes.

4.  Listen to your breathing. Draw in deep, full breaths. Let them out slowly, and feel yourself relax as you breathe out.

5.  Breathe in and tighten your leg muscles. Breathe out and relax. Breathe in and tighten your arm muscles. Breathe out and relax. Breathe in and tighten your face muscles. Breathe out and relax. Notice how calm they feel as you let them relax.

6.  Continue breathing in and out. Take slow, deep breaths.

7.  Think about being in a favorite place and being very relaxed and calm. Imagine putting your worries in a box on a high shelf.

8.  Stay quiet for a few minutes or as long as you need.

*Strong Kids—Grades 3–5: A Social and Emotional Learning Curriculum*
by Kenneth W. Merrell, with assistance from Dianna Carrizales, Laura Feuerborn,
Barbara A. Gueldner, and Oanh K. Tran © 2007 University of Oregon. All rights reserved.

 **Letting Go of Stress**

Name (optional): _____

1.  Write down times or situations where you felt stress.

    _____

    _____

    _____

2.  In class, we talked about strategies that can help you deal with stress. Some are listed below. Check off one or two relaxation strategies that you think you can try to use, or write in one that has worked for you.

    ☐  Talk to a trusted friend or adult

    ☐  Exercise

    ☐  Think positively about yourself and the situation

    ☐  Focus on your breathing and relaxing your muscles

    ☐  Identify your thinking error and reframe negative thoughts

    ☐  _____

3.  This week when I _____ (write in stressful situation)

    I will _____ (write in relaxation technique).

4.  After you have tried using one of the techniques you checked off above, write about how it worked for you. Did it work? What will you do next time in the same situation?

    ☐  It helped!

    _____

    _____

    ☐  I think I'll try something different next time.

    _____

    _____

## LESSON 11

### TEACHER NOTES

# Behavior Change

## *Setting Goals and Staying Active*

## ✶ Purpose

- To teach students goal setting and increasing positive activity as a means to a healthy life

## ✶ Objectives

- Students will be able to set short- and long-term practical and realistic goals.

- Students will learn that increasing and maintaining positive activities can help create a healthy lifestyle.

- Students will apply the procedures of positive goal setting to their lives.

- Students will generalize or apply this lesson to real-life situations.

---

**MATERIALS NEEDED:**

❑ Supplement 11.1 (overhead transparency and in-class handout)

❑ Supplement 11.2 (overhead transparency and in-class handout)

❑ Supplement 11.3 (homework handout)

**2–5 minutes**

# Review

To activate prior knowledge, review and discuss previous topics and main ideas. Obtain 3–5 adequate ideas. Discuss with students their responses to last week's homework assignment.

### Sample Script

*During our last meeting, we discussed relaxation and stress-relieving techniques. Raise your hand if you can tell me an important idea we learned in our last class.*

## Ideas Discussed in Lesson 10

- Stress is a normal part of being human.
- Describe the common signs of stress.
- Identify how you feel when stressed.
- Identifying positive and negative ways of reacting to stress.
- Evaluate whether a strategy will cause more stress in the future.
- Describe one relaxation exercise.

**5 minutes**

# Introduction

Communicate the lesson's purpose and objectives clearly. Introduce the concept of goal setting and creating an action plan to meet goals.

### Sample Script

*Today, we will learn how to set goals and accomplish them. We will learn how to use goals to change things in our lives that can be improved. Doing this successfully is called goal attainment. Together, we will practice goal setting by creating goals for ourselves and an action plan to make them happen.*

**5 minutes**

# Name and Define Skills

Use Supplement 11.1 as an overhead transparency and in-class handout to define and discuss the following important terms.

- *Goals*—specific objectives that you want to achieve (goals can be short and long term).
- *Goal setting*—defining a goal and creating a plan of action to achieve that goal
- *Goal attainment*—completing your action plan and achieving your goal

Provide examples and nonexamples of goal setting by using the following situation or using your own example.

*Sample Script*

*Suppose a student really wants to try out for a sports team at school. How would he go about making it onto the team? Let's discuss some actions he might take and decide whether they are examples of goal setting.*

*Situation 1 (Nonexample)*

*The student daydreams every day about his life after making the team.*

*Situation 2 (Nonexample)*

*The student draws soccer balls and famous soccer players while in class.*

*Situation 3 (Example)*

*The student finds out when tryouts or practices are.*

*Situation 4 (Example)*

*The student spends extra time at home practicing.*

# Steps to Goal Attainment

Convey the following main ideas to your students using your own words or the sample script.

- Goal attainment is an effective way to make change in your life.

- Maintaining positive hobbies and activities builds a stronger self.

- Goal attainment is flexible and subject to change.

- Goal setting is not the final step. It is important to follow through with your plan of action.

*Sample Script*

*You can use the goal-attainment process to improve or change parts of your life. When you do this, you might have more time to do activities you enjoy. You can also use the goal-attainment process to plan positive activities in your day. Many people who have positive activities in their routines are more likely to live healthy mental and physical lives. Part of the goal-attainment process is having a plan and following through with your plan.*

## Activity A: Six Steps to Goal Attainment

This section highlights six steps to setting and attaining goals. The examples provide the students with an opportunity to apply the lesson content to their own lives and to create their own specific goals. These examples can be modified to fit the needs and interests of your students. The six steps provide a foundation for students to use in the future when setting their own personal goals.

Use Supplement 11.2 as an overhead transparency and in-class handout to review the six steps of goal attainment. Provide an example for each step.

1. **Define your values**—What's important to you in the different areas of your life?

   - *Home example*—I don't like to make Mom mad at me.

- *School example*—I like to get good grades.

- *Free time example*—I want to make more friends.

2. **Create goals that reflect your values**—Write one item that you want to improve in each area.

   - *Home example*—I will keep my room clean.

   - *School example*—I want to get a better score on my next math quiz.

   - *Free time example*—I'll join after-school activities, such as playing sports.

3. **Brainstorm ways to reach your goal**—Who can help you? What tools and how much time will you need?

   - *Home example*—Every Sunday, I have some time to put my clothes away.

   - *School example*—I'll ask the math teacher for help.

   - *Free time example*—I will talk to other kids there.

4. **Evaluate your goal**—Is your goal practical? Is your goal realistic?

   - *Home example*—Yes, it is practical and realistic to clean my room once per week.

   - *School example*—No, it is not practical because I will not go to the math teacher by myself. Maybe I can ask a friend to go with me to see the teacher.

   - *Free time example*—Yes, it is practical and realistic to join a sports club.

5. **Implement your plan**—Write out a calendar. Tell someone you trust about your plan of action.

   - *Home example*—Mom will rent me a movie every Sunday that I clean my room.

   - *School example*—My friend also wants to get a better score on her math quiz. We can study together.

   - *Free time example*—I will attend the next sports activity after school.

6. **Check your progress**—Is your plan working? Do you need to make changes? Are there other goals you want to start working on?

   - *Home example*—Sunday is family day. Maybe I can make Saturday cleaning day.

   - *School example*—I got a better score on my math quiz with the help of my teacher and friend.

   - *Free time example*—I'm having fun with after-school activities and making more friends. I want to continue doing this.

## Activity B: Practice

In small groups or individually, ask students to generate their own goals and the steps of goal attainment they applied to their goal. Have students refer back to Supplement 11.2 as a guide. After a few minutes, ask if any students want to share their goals. If students do not want to share, that is okay. Continue sharing examples of steps and the overall process. Provide positive feedback for students who shared examples.

Review Supplement 11.2 as an overhead transparency while summarizing the six steps to goal attainment.

# Closure

Gather your students together, and review the lesson's main points.

- Define *goals*, *goal setting*, and *goal attainment*.
- List the steps to goal attainment.

### Sample Script

*Today, we learned a skill called goal attainment by practicing the steps with our own examples. I want you all to practice goal attainment at home, at school, and with your friends. The goal-attainment steps can also be used to increase positive activities in our regular schedules. Together, these skills help us build a healthy life.*

# Homework Handout

Pass out the homework handout, Supplement 11.3, Personal Goal Organizer. Tell students that they are to complete a personal goal organizer for home, school, and free time.

# Tips for Transfer Training

## Precorrect

Before class assignments, encourage students to set goals for themselves and to challenge themselves to achieve them. Encourage goals of words written, time taken, and problems completed in a certain time frame, and remind them how setting goals helps to stretch us to accomplish more and more.

## Remind

If students appear unmotivated during a class assignment, suggest goals that they can set for themselves, and ask them to challenge themselves to achieve these goals. For example, "Tuan, I see you haven't begun your writing assignment yet. Here's your goal: See if you can come up with 20 words of your assignment in the next 4 minutes. I'll be back in 4 minutes to see how you're doing."

## Reinforce

If you identify students using goal setting and attainment behaviors to accomplish tasks, specify their process, and compliment their behavior. For example, "Jenn, you told me you would try to get more problems correct this time, and you did it. Great job!"

 **Definitions**

### Goals

Specific objective that you want to achieve (goals can be short and long term)

### Goal setting

Defining a goal and creating a plan of action to achieve that goal

### Goal attainment

Completing your action plan and achieving your goal

 **Steps to Goal Attainment**

1.   Define your values.

2.   Create goals that reflect your values.

3.   Brainstorm ways to reach your goals.

4.   Evaluate your goals.

5.   Implement your plan.

6.   Check your progress.

*Strong Kids—Grades 3–5: A Social and Emotional Learning Curriculum*
by Kenneth W. Merrell, with assistance from Dianna Carrizales, Laura Feuerborn,
Barbara A. Gueldner, and Oanh K. Tran © 2007 University of Oregon. All rights reserved.          153

# ⊛ STRONG KIDS™  Personal Goal Organizer

Name (optional): _____

**Directions:** Complete this personal goal organizer for your activities at home, in school, and during your free time.

| | Home | School | Free time |
|---|---|---|---|
| **My values** | | | |
| **My goal** | | | |
| **Evaluate my goal** | ☐ Practical <br> ☐ Realistic | ☐ Practical <br> ☐ Realistic | ☐ Practical <br> ☐ Realistic |
| **Did I implement my plan?** | ☐ Yes <br> ☐ No | ☐ Yes <br> ☐ No | ☐ Yes <br> ☐ No |
| **Is my plan working?** | ☐ Yes. What goal can I work on now? <br> _____ <br> _____ <br> ☐ No. What changes can I make? <br> _____ <br> _____ | ☐ Yes. What goal can I work on now? <br> _____ <br> _____ <br> ☐ No. What changes can I make? <br> _____ <br> _____ | ☐ Yes. What goal can I work on now? <br> _____ <br> _____ <br> ☐ No. What changes can I make? <br> _____ <br> _____ |

STRONG K
LESSON

## LESSON 12

# Finishing UP!

## ⭐ Purpose

- To review the major concepts and skills in the *Strong Kids* curriculum

## ⭐ Objectives

- Students will identify comfortable and uncomfortable feelings and distinguish positive and negative examples of expressing feelings.

- Students will describe the Anger Model, the ABCDE Model of Learned Optimism, and the Problem-Solving Process.

- Students will identify common thinking errors and practice refuting negative thoughts.

- Students will identify signs of stress and strategies to relax.

- Students will describe the procedures of positive goal setting.

- Students will complete the assessment (optional); provide additional time if necessary.

| MATERIALS NEEDED |
| --- |
| ❑ Supplement 12.1 (overhead transparency) |

# Preparation

Prior to conducting the Finishing UP review lesson, it might be useful to review some of the lessons to refresh your memory. In addition, you will need the names and telephone numbers for mental health services, crisis hotlines, and other intervention services. These resources will be provided to students at the end the lesson. If you are not aware of this information, consider asking your supervisor, school counselor, or school psychologist. Many schools and agencies keep pamphlets with this type of information available for students.

# Introduction

Communicate the lesson's purpose and objectives clearly. Explain to your students that they will complete the final lesson of the *Strong Kids* curriculum today. Tell them that the topics they have been covering for the past several weeks will be reviewed and that they will complete an assessment exercise to measure what they have learned. Explain that they have learned many skills during this unit that are vital to their social and emotional health, and they will have opportunities to use these skills throughout their lives.

### Sample Script

*Today, we will finish the Strong Kids unit that we have been working on for the past several weeks. We have discussed how to understand our feelings and the feelings of others. We have also discussed how to solve problems, how to set goals, and how to think in a way that helps us in life to make better choices. We know that sometimes we encounter serious problems in our lives and that we may need help to solve these problems. Today, we will review everything we have learned. We will discuss what to do if problems ever get serious.*

# Review of *Strong Kids*

Use this lesson as an opportunity to discuss any terms or concepts that may be relevant to your class at this time, to revisit any of the ideas that needed expansion during the term, or to simply refresh the ideas.

*Note:* If you conducted a pretest assessment before or during Lesson 1 and intend to conduct follow-up assessment of the *Strong Kids* curriculum at the end of this lesson, you will need to reserve enough instructional time to do so. If you do not intend to conduct follow-up assessment, extend this instruction portion of the lesson with review as needed.

Use Supplement 12.1 as an overhead transparency. Read through the names of the lessons, and ask students to recall main points from each lesson. For your reference, the main ideas for the lessons are provided on the following pages. In addition, sample hints are provided to spark students' memories about the lessons. It may be useful to look at Lessons 2–11 prior to this discussion to familiarize yourself with some of the concepts that were presented. If necessary, retrieve Supplements from specific lessons to reteach relevant terms.

- Understanding Your Feelings (1 and 2)
- Dealing with Anger
- Understanding Other People's Feelings
- Clear Thinking (1 and 2)
- The Power of Positive Thinking
- Solving People Problems
- Letting Go of Stress
- Behavior Change: Setting Goals and Staying Active

### Sample Script

*We are going to review the main ideas from each lesson. Who can tell me a main idea from Lessons 2 and 3, Understanding Your Feelings?*

Encourage students to raise their hands and share some of the ideas that have been discussed. Alternately, consider assigning individual lessons to small groups of students and then having the groups report the key ideas to the class verbally or on a small poster, as part of a guided discussion activity.

## Lessons 2 and 3: Understanding Your Feelings (1 and 2)

Prompt students to discuss the main ideas for this lesson.

- *Emotions*—Internal feelings about different situations. Are all emotions okay? Yes, but there are positive (okay) and negative (not okay) ways of expressing feelings.
- *Comfortable feelings*—happy, excited
- *Uncomfortable feelings*—worried, frustrated

### Sample Hint

*We talked about different situations and how you would feel if it really happened to you. For example, how would you feel if your friend broke your favorite CD or you had to show your parents a bad report card?*

## Lesson 4: Dealing with Anger

Prompt students to discuss the main ideas for this lesson.

- *Anger*—a powerful emotion of extreme unhappiness and dislike toward someone or something when you feel threatened or harmed
- *Aggression*—forceful or oppositional behavior or words that cause physical or emotional harm to others, yourself, or property
- *Anger management*—choosing appropriate behaviors when you are angry
- *The Anger Model*—1) trigger, 2) interpretation, 3) emotional reaction, 4) decision, 5) behavior, and 6) consequence
- Anger control skills

### Sample Hint

*We talked about counting backwards quietly from 10 to 1 and about self-talk, if-then statements, and self-evaluation.*

## Lesson 5: Understanding Other People's Feelings

Prompt students to discuss the main ideas for this lesson.

- *Empathy*—understanding another person's feelings or emotions
- *Perspective*—feelings and opinions each person has about an experience
- *Clues/cues*—signals or signs that tell you something about another person

### Sample Hint

*We role-played different behaviors to guess people's emotions.*

## Lesson 6: Clear Thinking 1

Prompt students to discuss the main ideas for this lesson.

- Awareness of the range of emotions
- *Binocular vision*—looking at things in a way that exaggerates them
- *Black-and-white thinking*—looking at things in extreme ways, using words like *never, always, all, none, good,* and *bad*
- *Dark glasses*—thinking about only the negative parts of things
- *Fortune-telling*—making predictions about what will happen in the future without enough evidence
- *Making it personal*—blaming yourself for things that are not your fault
- *Blame game*—blaming others for things that you should take responsibility for

### Sample Hint

*We talked about the thermometer and how high or low our feelings were on the thermometer.*

## Lesson 7: Clear Thinking 2

Prompt students to discuss the main ideas for this lesson.

- Changing the negative thought patterns discussed in Lesson 6
- Evidence for or against thinking errors
- *Reframing*—looking at a situation in a more realistic or positive way

### Sample Hint

*We talked about looking for evidence "for" or "against" our thoughts and then making a decision if the evidence was reasonable.*

## Lesson 8: The Power of Positive Thinking

Prompt students to discuss the main ideas for this lesson.

- *Self-control*—the ability to control your own behavior, especially in terms of your actions and impulses
- *Optimism*—believing, expecting, or hoping that things will turn out well
- *The ABCDE Model of Learned Optimism*—Adversity, Belief, Consequence, Deciding, and Energy

### Sample Hint

*We talked about the ABCDE Model of Learned Optimism.*

- *A was Any problem that you can't control.*
- *B was the Bad thoughts that make you think things are your fault.*
- *C was that Crummy feeling that gets in your head and makes things feel worse.*
- *D was the positive Decision not to accept the crummy thoughts!*
- *E was the great part where you got to Enjoy the idea that you can control what you think about yourself.*

## Lesson 9: Solving People Problems

Prompt students to discuss the main ideas for this lesson.

- *Conflict or problem*—a disagreement or something that doesn't match or work well together
- *Resolve*—to fix, mend, or solve
- *Resolution*—the part where you are finding a solution, or resolving a problem
- *Problem solving*—finding some way to work out a problem
- *Problem-Solving Model*—1) identify the problem, 2) brainstorm solutions, 3) choose a solution, and 4) make an agreement

### Sample Hint

*We went through the problem-solving steps, where we identified the problem, brainstormed solutions, chose a solution, and then made an agreement.*

## Lesson 10: Letting Go of Stress

Prompt students to discuss the main ideas for this lesson.

- *Stress*—a feeling of being overwhelmed, demonstrated by body signals: teeth clench up, fists clench, muscles tighten, scared, worried, nervous, feel like you can't do it, body or hands shake, irritability, and feeling tired
- Relaxation techniques

### Sample Hint

*We found our quiet spaces and closed our eyes and practiced deep breathing and sitting quietly.*

### Lesson 11: Behavior Change: Setting Goals and Staying Active

Prompt students to discuss the main ideas for this lesson.

- *Goals*—something specific that you want to achieve (sooner or later)

- *Goal setting*—deciding on a goal and setting up a plan that can help to get you there

- *Goal attainment*—finally achieving your goal!

- Steps to goal attainment

  *Sample Hint:*

  *We talked about the six steps to achieving your goals: 1) define your values and decide what is important to you, 2) create goals that match what is important to you, 3) brainstorm ideas on how to reach your goals, 4) think about your goals and make sure they are reasonable and not too difficult, 5) put your plan into action, and 6) regularly check the progress of your plan.*

## Options for Students Experiencing Significant Problems

Explain to students that they have learned important skills during this unit but that these skills may not be enough help for serious life problems.

*Sample Script*

*We have learned important skills that will help you in many situations, but sometimes we encounter serious problems in our lives that we may need help to solve. If a problem ever gets serious, there are always people you can turn to for help.*

### Activity A

List the people in the school *and* community whom students can turn to for help. Help students generate names if they can't think of any (e.g., parent, other adult family members, a close adult friend or neighbor, clergy person, principal, teacher, counselor, school psychologist). Also, include information on locating mental health services, crisis lines, and so forth. List the resources on the board or overhead projector.

*Sample Script*

- *Who are some people at school whom you can turn to for help? What are their names?*

- *Who are the other people in the community whom you can turn to for help? If you know them, what are their names?*

- *Who is someone in your home whom you can turn to for help?*

- *We have named many adults at school, in the community, and at home whom you can talk to if a problem ever gets serious. Think about the person whom you trust the most, and remember that you can talk to that person if you need help.*

## 15 minutes **Optional Assessments**

If you administered pretests from the *Strong Kids* web site (http://strongkids. uoregon.edu) during Lesson 1, now is the time to administer these tests again so that you can determine how effective *Strong Kids* was at increasing students' knowledge and enhancing their emotional resiliency. It will take approximately 15 minutes to take these tests.

## 5–10 minutes **Closure**

Gather your students together, and review the main points. Remind students to contact adults listed if they have additional questions or concerns. Congratulate students on finishing *Strong Kids*.

### Sample Script

*Today, we reviewed everything we learned in Strong Kids. As we have worked through Strong Kids, we have shared stories with each other. Remember that stories are personal, and, even though today is the last day of Strong Kids, we will remember not to share other students' stories with anyone outside of the group. By keeping others' stories to yourself, you will be respecting others.*

*Today, we also reviewed what to do if a problem ever gets serious. You know whom you can turn to if you need help.*

*Congratulations on finishing Strong Kids! You have learned many important new skills. Your skills have built up your emotional strength, and they will continue to be valuable as you become an adult. You will have opportunities to use your skills to be emotionally healthy throughout your life.*

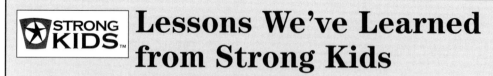

# Lessons We've Learned from Strong Kids

Understanding Your Feelings (1 and 2)


Dealing with Anger


Understanding Other People's Feelings


Clear Thinking (1 and 2)


The Power of Positive Thinking


Solving People Problems


Letting Go of Stress


Behavior Change: Setting Goals and Staying Active

# *Strong Kids* Booster
## *Pulling It All Together*

**TEACHER NOTES**

_____

_____

_____

_____

_____

_____

_____

_____

_____

_____

_____

_____

_____

_____

_____

_____

_____

_____

_____

_____

## Purpose

- To remind students of the main ideas covered in *Strong Kids* and provide opportunities for review and practice

## Objectives

- Students will review the range and breadth of normal emotions.

- Students will practice identifying emotions.

- Students will review the skills necessary to change and control their emotions.

| MATERIALS NEEDED |
| --- |

- ❏ Supplement A.1 (overhead transparency)
- ❏ Supplement A.2 (overhead transparency)
- ❏ Supplement A.3 (overhead transparency)
- ❏ Supplements from previous lessons as needed
- ❏ Names and telephone numbers of local mental health service organizations

*Note:* This booster lesson may be taught in one or two sessions and adapted as needed

# Preparation

Determine the skills and activities that you want to focus on most strongly, and decide whether to conduct the booster lesson in one session or to divide it into two sessions. Choose from the four activities provided in the lesson to practice the skills you consider to be most relevant for your students.

- Situations and feelings list
- Feelings jar
- Situations and empathy statements
- Activity sheets

   Refer to the lesson titles and questions as you discuss the major themes.

# Introduction

Communicate the lesson's purpose and objectives clearly. Review concepts from Lessons 1–11 about emotions, thinking, and behavior.

### Sample Script

*Today, we are going to review some of the things we learned from the Strong Kids program we completed [last month]. Once again, we are going to talk about our emotions, thoughts, and behavior.*

# Review of Topics

Use Supplement A.1 as an overhead transparency to guide this activity. Read the sample script, and discuss the main points for Lessons 1–11. Spend about 3 minutes on each lesson review. Provide the main points to jog the students' memory, and then solicit one or two comments to determine the students' familiarity with the concepts. Hints are provided as reminders if the students are unable to remember anything from the lesson.

### Sample Script

*I am going to quickly read through the main points from the Strong Kids lessons that we covered, and then I'm going to see what you remember from each of them. Try to remember as many important points as you can, and afterward we'll have some opportunities to think about our feelings and everything we learned in Strong Kids.*

## Lesson 1: About *Strong Kids:* Emotional Strength Training

### Sample Script

*We learned the rules for participation in the Strong Kids program.*

Main ideas:

- Respect others (listen quietly when someone is speaking).

- Come prepared (do homework assignments).
- Personal things stay in the group.

## Lessons 2 and 3: Understanding Your Feelings 1 and 2

### Sample Script

*We learned how to identify feelings and discussed whether they were comfortable or uncomfortable. We also talked about different ways of expressing feelings; some ways were appropriate, and some ways were not appropriate.*

Main ideas:

- Everyone has emotions or feelings, and it is okay to have any feeling.
- Emotions arise because of different situations.
- Emotions can be used to communicate how I feel and how others feel.
- There are different ways of showing feelings.
- Other people may not feel the same way I do about everything.
- I can do things to change how I feel and how others feel.

### Sample Hint

*Do you remember how we talked about all of the different situations and about how you would feel if it really happened to you? So, for example, how would you feel if your friend was talking about you behind your back or if you didn't get invited to do something you really wanted to do?*

Statements from Supplement A.2, the Situations and Feelings List, can be used for discussion and examples. For example, numbers 4, 5, 14, 15, 16, 17, 18, 20, 21, and 22 would be appropriate to illustrate Lessons 2 and 3.

## Lesson 4: Dealing with Anger

### Sample Script

*We learned about a way to look at what happens when we get angry as a series of steps. The Anger Model is 1) trigger, 2) interpretation, 3) emotional reaction, 4) decision, 5) behavior, and 6) consequence.*

Main ideas:

- Anger is a necessary and natural reaction.
- Aggression is not the best way to deal with anger.
- There are other ways to react to anger.
- What are the steps of the Anger Model?
- What are anger control skills?

### Sample Hint

*Do you remember how we talked about counting backwards quietly from 10 to 1, and about self-talk, if-then statements, and self-evaluation?*

Statements from Supplement A.2, the Situations and Feelings List, can be used to role-play about managing anger skills. Use relevant examples from the list to role-play, using the anger management model. For example, numbers 3, 9, and 21 would be appropriate in illustrating Lesson 4.

## Lesson 5: Understanding Other People's Feelings

### Sample Script

*We learned about empathy, how to recognize other people's feelings, and to take their perspectives. We looked for clues or cues to try to figure out how someone is feeling.*

Main ideas:

- It might be possible to tell someone's feelings by looking for visual clues.

- People may or may not share the same perspective in the same situation.

- It is important to listen to others to find out how they are feeling.

### Sample Hint

*Do you remember how we role-played different behaviors to guess people's emotions?*

Statements from Supplement A.2, the Situations and Feelings List, can be used to discuss how someone else might feel in that same situation. For example, numbers 16, 18, and 22 would be appropriate to illustrate Lesson 5.

## Lesson 6: Clear Thinking 1

### Sample Script

*We learned how to identify negative thought patterns and thinking errors.*

Main ideas:

- Emotions can be experienced to varying degrees, from low to high.

- Thoughts usually happen at about the same time as feelings.

- Sometimes thinking errors occur during negative thought patterns.

- The thinking errors are 1) making it personal, 2) fortune-telling, 3) binocular vision, 4) dark glasses, 5) black-and-white thinking, 6) blame game.

### Sample Hint

*Do you remember how we talked about the thermometer and how high or low our feelings were on the thermometer?*

Statements from Supplement A.2, the Situations and Feelings List, can be used to discuss if any negative thoughts/thinking errors might occur in that situation and how you could change the negative thoughts. For example, numbers 11, 12, 13, 16, and 19 may be appropriate to illustrate Lesson 6.

## Lesson 7: Clear Thinking 2

### Sample Script

*We learned strategies to change thinking errors and negative thoughts by 1) using evidence, 2) reframing, and 3) being realistic.*

Main ideas:

- The steps of Changing Thinking Errors are 1) identify negative thoughts, 2) look for evidence for or against, 3) decide if there was a thinking error, and 4) use reframing to think about it realistically or more positively.

### Sample Hint

*Do you remember how we talked about looking for evidence "for" or "against" our thoughts, and then making a decision if the evidence was reasonable?*

Statements from Supplement A.2, the Situations and Feelings List, can be used to reframe negative thinking based on supporting evidence. For example, numbers 11, 12, 13, 16, and 19 may be appropriate to illustrate Lesson 7.

## Lesson 8: The Power of Positive Thinking

### Sample Script

*We learned how to become a person who thinks positively by recognizing and changing the way we look at adversity or problems. We used the ABCDE model to think positively:*

- *A—Any problem that I can't control.*
- *B—Bad thoughts that make me think things are my fault.*
- *C—Crummy feelings that I get in my head that make me feel worse.*
- *D—Decide not to accept the crummy thoughts.*
- *E—Enjoy the idea that I can control what I think about myself.*

Main ideas:

- Experiencing negative thoughts is normal.
- The ABCDE model can change negative thoughts into positive thinking.

### Sample Hint

*Let's review the ABCDE Model of Learned Optimism. Do you remember how it worked?*

Statements from Supplement A.2, the Situations and Feelings List, can be used to illustrate situations that are out of a person's control and that the steps of positive thinking would address. For example, number 11 may be used to illustrate Lesson 8.

## Lesson 9: Solving People Problems

### Sample Script

*We learned about conflicts and how to resolve them peacefully by using a problem-solving strategy.*

Main ideas:

- The steps of the Problem-Solving Model are 1) identify the problem, 2) brainstorm solutions, 3) choose one of the solutions, and 4) make an agreement.

- Conflict resolution requires patience and creativity.

- What statements can you use during conflict resolution?

### Sample Hint

*Do you remember how we went through the problem-solving steps where we identified the problem, brainstormed solutions, chose a solution, and then made an agreement?*

Statements from Supplement A.2, the Situations and Feelings List, can be used to determine situations involving other people that can be problem-solved. Look at the situation from both sides if possible. For example, numbers 9 and 11 may be appropriate to illustrate Lesson 9.

## Lesson 10: Letting Go of Stress

### Sample Script

*We learned some ways to recognize signs of stress, and some ways to reduce stress with the way we think and with some simple exercises.*

Main ideas:

- Some feelings in your body that go with stress are hands or body shakes, fists clench, teeth and jaws clench up, muscles tighten, feels like you can't do it, fatigue, irritability, scared/worried/nervous.

- Some ways to relieve stress in your body are to talk about your problem with a friend, do something active, face your fears, and try a relaxation activity in a quiet place.

### Sample Hint

*Do you remember how we found our quiet spaces and closed our eyes and practiced deep breathing, and sitting quietly?*

Statements from Supplement A.2, the Situations and Feelings List, can be used to discuss signs of stress and ways to relieve it. For example, numbers 1, 2, 5, 14, 15, and 21 may be appropriate to illustrate Lesson 10.

## Lesson 11: Behavior Change: Setting Goals and Staying Active

### Sample Script

*We talked about how to set practical goals and how to take steps toward them.*

Main ideas:

- What is a goal, and what is your goal?

- How do you set a goal, and how do you achieve a goal?

- The steps to goal attainment are 1) define your values, 2) create goals that reflect your values, 3) brainstorm ways to reach your goal, 4) evaluate your goal, 5) take action, and 6) check your progress.

### Sample Hint

*Do you remember how we talked about the six steps to achieving your goals, where you 1) define your values and decide what is important to you, 2) create goals that match what is important to you, 3) brainstorm for ideas on how to reach your goals, 4) think about your goals and make sure they are reasonable and not too difficult, 5) put your plan into action, and 6) check on the progress of your plan every so often?*

Statements from Supplement A.2, the Situations and Feelings List, can be used to discuss places where someone can use the steps to goal attainment to improve their feelings. For example, numbers 1, 2, 6, 7, 8, 10, 14, and 21 may be appropriate to illustrate Lesson 11.

**5–15 minutes** ## Practice Activities

Choose from the following four activities to practice the skills you consider to be most relevant for your students.

- Activity A: Situations and feelings list

- Activity B: Feelings jar

- Activity C: Situations and empathy statements

- Activity D: Activity sheets

### Activity A: Situations and Feelings List

Supplement A.2 provides situations and feelings that students could have at any point in time. Each item corresponds with a number from 1 to 22. Following each situation or feeling is the number of the lesson that corresponds with some of the issues that might surround that situation or feeling. Use these lesson indicators as a guide, but also see if anyone can provide different perspectives on the situation or feeling and encourage dialogue. Discussion questions provided on Supplement A.3 can be used to guide students through each example.

Using a fast pace, choose a student and ask him or her to give you a number from 1 to 22. Find the situation or feeling that corresponds with the number on the list, and facilitate a discussion regarding this situation or feeling, highlighting main points from the lessons in *Strong Kids*.

### Sample Script

*Let's look at examples of situations and feelings that students might have. As we talk about these feelings, think about how you would respond, now that you have participated in the Strong Kids lessons. [Student name], choose a number between 1 and 22. Okay, let's look at this feeling.*

As the situations or feelings are read, lead the discussion with questions such as the following:

- What is the feeling?

- Is it comfortable or uncomfortable?

- What strategies can be used to change the feeling if it is uncomfortable?

## Activity B: Feelings Jar

Ask students to write a short description of a time when they felt a particular feeling and why they felt a certain way. For example, one student might write, "Today, another student said she liked my new shoes. This compliment made me feel happy." This is an example of a comfortable feeling. Another student might write, "Today, it looked like I was going to be picked last for the basketball team. I was nervous until the captain called my name." This is an example of an uncomfortable feeling. Read several examples, using the students' situations as a discussion topic. For advanced students, descriptions could include the situation, the feeling it generated, and what action they took.

Discussion questions provided on Supplement A.3 can be used to guide students through each example. Use questions such as the following:

- What are some of the feelings in this situation?

- Is the feeling comfortable or uncomfortable?

- Is this the only way to look at the situation?

- If the feeling is uncomfortable, how is this individual handling the situation (e.g., negative thinking, inappropriate behavior)?

- What other ways are there to handle this situation?

- Which *Strong Kids* lesson does this remind you of?

## Activity C: Situations and Empathy Statements

As a class or in small groups, ask the students to discuss the following situations, and see how many of the *Strong Kids* ideas they are able to identify as a class or in small groups. Instruct students to think critically about all of the details presented in each situation, including everyone's perspective. Ask students to give the main character the benefit of the doubt. Then, ask students to identify the main character's point of view and ways the character could show empathy. Doing so will help students view the situation from several perspectives.

Discussion questions provided on Supplement A.3 can be used to guide students through each example. Relevant supplements from Lessons 2 through 11 are referenced if you wish to review these with the class to provide additional practice for each situation. Use questions such as the following:

- What are some of the feelings in this situation?

- Were the feelings comfortable or uncomfortable?

- Is this the only way to look at the situation?
- If the feeling is uncomfortable, how is this individual handling the situation (e.g., negative thinking, inappropriate behavior)?
- What other ways are there to handle this situation?
- Which *Strong Kids* lesson does this remind you of?

### Situation 1

*Megan is getting a new stepdad. She doesn't like him much. His jokes aren't funny. He talks too loud, and she liked it better when it was just her and her mom. Megan believes that if she could get better grades or behave a little better at home and school, her mom would be happier and things could stay the way they are. It's hard to be good all the time, and it's hard to keep her grades up, so Megan feels really bad about what's going to happen. Her mom is getting married anyway, and it will be all her fault.*

Lessons indicated:

- Understanding Your Feelings 1 (Supplements 2.1 and 2.2)
- Understanding Other People's Feelings (Supplement 5.2)
- Clear Thinking 1 and 2 (Supplements 6.1, 6.2, 7.2, 7.3, and 7.4)
- The Power of Positive Thinking (Supplements 8.1, 8.2, and 8.3)
- Letting Go of Stress (Supplements 10.1 and 10.2)
- Behavior Change: Setting Goals and Staying Active (Supplements 11.1 and 11.2)

Prompt students to generate ideas about the situation and how to problem-solve using the strategies learned.

### Situation 2

*Pedro was caught chewing gum at school. The teacher saw him and gave him a referral because it had happened before. Some of Pedro's friends overheard him being reprimanded. One of them laughed. Pedro decided to hang out on his own for the rest of the day. He is thinking about getting some new friends.*

Lessons indicated:

- Understanding Your Feelings 1 (Supplements 2.1 and 2.2)
- Dealing with Anger (Supplements 4.1, 4.2, and 4.3)
- Understanding Other People's Feelings (Supplement 5.2)
- Clear Thinking 1 and 2 (Supplements 6.1, 6.2, 7.2, 7.3, and 7.4)
- Solving People Problems (Supplements 9.1, 9.2, and 9.3)

Prompt students to generate ideas about the situation and how to problem-solve using the strategies learned.

### Situation 3

*Mika's brother used his own money to buy a Play Station game. Mika had not saved his money but he really wanted to play the game. He waited until he thought his brother was not around and then began to play the game. Just as Mika was about to get to an important level of the game, his brother came in, grabbed the control, and turned off the game. Mika shoved his brother and left the room.*

Lessons indicated:

- Understanding Your Feelings 1 (Supplement 2.1)
- Dealing with Anger (Supplements 4.1, 4.2, and 4.3)
- Understanding Other People's Feelings (Supplement 5.2)
- Clear Thinking 1 and 2 (Supplements 6.1, 6.2, 7.2, 7.3, and 7.4)
- Solving People Problems (Supplements 9.1, 9.2, and 9.3)
- Letting Go of Stress (Supplements 10.1 and 10.2)
- Behavior Change: Setting Goals and Staying Active (Supplements 11.1 and 11.2)

Prompt students to generate ideas about the situation and how to problem-solve using the strategies learned.

### Activity D: Activity Sheets

Use any of the activity sheets provided in the curriculum to practice any skills that appear to need additional review.

## Identifying Student Resources

Explain to your students that they have learned important skills during this unit but that these skills may not be enough help for them if they encounter serious life problems.

*Sample Script*

*We have learned important skills that will help you in many situations, but sometimes we have serious problems in our lives that we may need help to solve. If a problem ever gets serious, there are always people you can turn to for help.*

List the people in the school/community whom they can turn to for help or use the following brief discussion activity.

*Sample Script*

*Who are some people at school you can ask for help?*

List the names of identified school personnel on the board or overhead projector. Help students generate names if they get stuck (e.g., principal, teacher, counselor, school psychologist).

*Sample Script*

*We have named many adults at school whom you can talk to if a problem ever gets serious. There are also people outside of school whom you can turn to for help. Who are some of these people?*

List the names of identified community personnel on the board or overhead projector. Help students generate names if they get stuck (e.g., parent, other adult family member, a close adult friend or neighbor, clergyperson). Include information on locating mental health services (e.g., crisis line telephone numbers and addresses).

### Sample Script

*We have named many adults at home or in our community whom you can talk to if a problem ever gets serious. Now, think about the person whom you trust the most, and write down that person's name. I want you to consider these people to talk to if you ever have any questions or are experiencing serious problems.*

# Closure

Tell students that this is the last day of *Strong Kids*. Remind them to keep other students' stories confidential.

### Sample Script

*Today, we reviewed everything we learned in Strong Kids. As we have worked through Strong Kids, we have shared stories with each other. Remember that stories are personal, and even though today is the last day of Strong Kids, we will remember not to share other students' stories with anyone outside of the group. By keeping others' stories to yourself, you will be respecting others. Look for opportunities to use the skills you learned in Strong Kids to be emotionally healthy throughout your life. Everyone did a great job participating in Strong Kids.*

 **Lessons from Strong Kids**

1.  About *Strong Kids:* Emotional Strength Training

2.  Understanding Your Feelings 1

3.  Understanding Your Feelings 2

4.  Dealing with Anger

5.  Understanding Other People's Feelings

6.  Clear Thinking 1

7.  Clear Thinking 2

8.  The Power of Positive Thinking

9.  Solving People Problems

10. Letting Go of Stress

11. Behavior Change: Setting Goals and Staying Active

12. Finishing UP!

*Strong Kids—Grades 3–5: A Social and Emotional Learning Curriculum*
by Kenneth W. Merrell, with assistance from Dianna Carrizales, Laura Feuerborn,
Barbara A. Gueldner, and Oanh K. Tran © 2007 University of Oregon. All rights reserved.

 **The Situations and Feelings List**

| Situations and feelings | Lesson |
|---|---|
| 1.  My hands shake when I have to take a test. | 10, 11 |
| 2.  I feel nervous all the time. | 10, 11 |
| 3.  I get really angry at my brother or sister. He or she makes me want to punch a wall. | 4 |
| 4.  I am getting better at skateboarding/guitar/piano. | 2, 3 |
| 5.  I am looking forward to vacation. | 2, 3, 10 |
| 6.  I need money. | 11 |
| 7.  I hate my clothes. | 11 |
| 8.  I want to change the way I look. | 11 |
| 9.  I am mad at my parents. | 4, 9 |
| 10.  I need a new bike. | 11 |
| 11.  I'm having problems with my friends. | 6, 7, 8, 9 |
| 12.  My problems are so much bigger than this. | 6, 7, 12 |
| 13.  My parents are getting divorced/separating. | 6, 7, 12 |
| 14.  I graduate soon or am transferring schools. | 2, 3, 10, 11 |
| 15.  I would like to go to college. | 2, 3, 10 |
| 16.  My parents are planning college for me. | 2, 3, 5, 6, 7 |
| 17.  I got a job. | 2, 3 |
| 18.  I have to babysit my younger brothers or sisters. | 2, 3, 5 |
| 19.  I am getting a new stepmom or stepdad. | 6, 7 |
| 20.  I got good grades. | 2, 3 |
| 21.  I got bad grades. | 2, 3, 4, 10, 11 |
| 22.  I am not the teacher's favorite. | 2, 3, 5 |

# ★ STRONG KIDS™ Discussion Questions

1. What are some of the feelings in this situation?

2. Is the feeling comfortable or uncomfortable?

3. Is this the only way to look at the situation?

4. If the feeling is uncomfortable, how is this individual handling the situation?

5. What kind of thinking is he or she using? Negative or positive?

6. What other ways are there to handle this situation?

7. Which *Strong Kids* lesson does this remind you of?